Issues

Annual Index
2009

Your one-stop reference guide to the ever-popular Issues series!

Complete A-Z index listings for all 67 Issues titles currently in print

A fully comprehensive research tool for your students

Now extended for even greater coverage!

First published by Independence
The Studio, High Green, Great Shelford
Cambridge CB22 5EG

ISBN 978 1 86168 522 3

Compiled by
Ann Shooter

Edited and typeset by
Lisa Firth

Printed in Great Britain
MWL Print Group Ltd

Cover
The illustration on the front cover is by
Don Hatcher.

A

A8 countries migrants and homelessness **130**.19
A-levels (Advanced Level) **139**.4
  'dumbing down' claims **139**.19-20
  and gender **139**.10; **154**.22-3, 26
  results **139**.18
  science **139**.21
abortion **171**.1-39
  access to abortion services **171**.33
    at GP surgeries **171**.25-6
    online advice **171**.36
  after-effects **171**.3, 4-5
  arguments against (pro-life) **171**.21-3, 31
  arguments for (pro-choice) **171**.32-3
  attitudes to **171**.8
  definition **152**.2
  early medical abortion **171**.26
  failure **171**.2-3, 4
  home abortions **171**.35-6
  and humanism **171**.19-21
  and the law **171**.1, 5-7
    and doctors' objections to abortions **171**.27-8
    Northern Ireland **171**.15-16
    and religion **171**.18
    worldwide **171**.11-12
  methods
    medical abortion ('the abortion pill') **171**.2, 35, 36
    surgical abortion (vacuum aspiration) **171**.2
    unsafe methods **171**.12
  reasons for abortions **171**.1
    disability **171**.22
    rape **171**.21-2
    to save mother's life **171**.23
  religious positions on **171**.17-19
  risks **171**.3, 4-5
  safety, worldwide **171**.11-12
  statistics **171**.11-12; **173**.3, 9
  success rate **171**.2-3
  and teenage pregnancies **133**.2, 9; **173**.3, 9
    under 16s **133**.2
  time limit
    public opinion **171**.30
    reasons to keep at 24 weeks **171**.32-4
    reasons to reduce **171**.31
    women's opinions **171**.29
absenteeism **107**.6-8, 18
  from school, gender differences **154**.25
absolute human rights **167**.2, 4
abstinence education **173**.37
abuse
  as cause of self-harm **136**.1
  effect on children **166**.35
  and young people **155**.19-26
abusers
  domestic, help for **155**.33-4
  see also paedophiles
academic achievement *see* educational achievement
academic freedom **121**.8-9
academies **139**.14-16
  Special Educational Needs provision **135**.36
Acceptable Behaviour Contracts (ABCs) **177**.8
access, disabled people **135**.3
  and Disability Discrimination Act **135**.22
access to children *see* contact

Volume numbers appear first (in bold) followed by page numbers; a change in volume number is preceded by a semi-colon.

Vol. 76 The Water Crisis
Vol. 78 Threatened Species
Vol. 81 Alternative Therapies
Vol. 88 Food and Nutrition
Vol. 89 Refugees
Vol. 97 Energy Matters
Vol. 99 Exploited Children
Vol. 100 Stress and Anxiety
Vol. 107 Work Issues
Vol. 116 Grief and Loss
Vol. 118 Focus on Sport
Vol. 119 Transport Trends
Vol. 121 The Censorship Debate
Vol. 124 Parenting Issues
Vol. 125 Understanding Depression
Vol. 127 Eating Disorders
Vol. 128 The Cannabis Issue
Vol. 129 Gambling Trends
Vol. 130 Homelessness
Vol. 133 Teen Pregnancy and Lone Parents
Vol. 134 Customers and Consumerism
Vol. 135 Coping with Disability
Vol. 136 Self-Harm

Vol. 138 A Genetically Modified Future?
Vol. 139 The Education Problem
Vol. 140 Vegetarian and Vegan Diets
Vol. 141 Mental Health
Vol. 142 Media Issues
Vol. 143 Problem Drinking
Vol. 144 The Cloning Debate
Vol. 145 Smoking Trends
Vol. 146 Sustainability and Environment
Vol. 147 The Terrorism Problem
Vol. 148 Religious Beliefs
Vol. 149 A Classless Society?
Vol. 150 Migration and Population
Vol. 151 Climate Change
Vol. 152 Euthanasia and the Right to Die
Vol. 153 Sexual Orientation and Society
Vol. 154 The Gender Gap
Vol. 155 Domestic Abuse
Vol. 156 Travel and Tourism
Vol. 157 The Problem of Globalisation
Vol. 158 The Internet Revolution
Vol. 159 An Ageing Population
Vol. 160 Poverty and Exclusion

Vol. 161 Waste Issues
Vol. 162 Staying Fit
Vol. 163 Drugs in the UK
Vol. 164 The AIDS Crisis
Vol. 165 Bullying Issues
Vol. 166 Marriage and Cohabitation
Vol. 167 Our Human Rights
Vol. 168 Privacy and Surveillance
Vol. 169 The Animal Rights Debate
Vol. 170 Body Image and Self-Esteem
Vol. 171 Abortion – Rights and Ethics
Vol. 172 Racial and Ethnic Discrimination
Vol. 173 Sexual Health
Vol. 174 Selling Sex
Vol. 175 Citizenship and Participation
Vol. 176 Health Issues for Young People
Vol. 177 Crime in the UK
Vol. 178 Reproductive Ethics
Vol. 179 Tackling Child Abuse
Vol. 180 Money and Finances
Vol. 181 The Housing Issue

access courses **139**.30
access rights, fathers **133**.39
accident warning devices, cars **119**.19
accidents
    alcohol-related **176**.15
    child labour and work-related **99**.1
    falls, older people **159**.4, 6
    road accidents, children **119**.5, 28, 30-31
    young people **176**.4
achievement *see* educational achievement
acid rain **76**.11
acne **176**.20
action plan orders **177**.17
active euthanasia **152**.5
active traffic management **119**.37-8
activists and the media **142**.10
activity
    as help for depression **125**.3, 39
    physical *see* exercise
Acts of Parliament **131**.24
acupressure **81**.1, 3
acupuncture **81**.5-6, 14, 23, 36
addictions **141**.9-10
    cannabis **128**.2, 8, 15
    gambling *see* compulsive gambling
    drugs **163**.2
    to the Internet **142**.37; **158**.38-9
    nicotine **145**.26
        children **145**.2-3; **176**.13
    online gaming **158**.39
    to self-harm **136**.9
    shopping **134**.13-14
addictiveness of gambling **129**.30
ADD *see* attention deficit disorder
ADHD (attention deficit and hyperactivity disorder)
        141.19; **176**.30
    and eating disorders **127**.10
adoption **178**.14-16
    and father's rights **133**.39
    process **133**.8-9
    same-sex couples **153**.31-2, 34; **178**.9-10
adrenaline and nicotine **145**.26

adult children
    living with parents **180**.23; **181**.4-5
    parental interference **124**.14-15
    supported by parents **124**.3
adult literacy rates, and child labour **99**.11-12
adulterous consumption **161**.8-9
adultery **166**.13-14
adultescents **124**.3
advance directives (living wills) **152**.2, 35-6
    and the Mental Capacity Act **152**.37
advance fee scams **134**.26-7
Advanced Extension Awards (AEA) **139**.18
Advanced Highers **139**.4
advertising **134**.7-1
    anti-smoking **145**.18-19
    benefits of **134**.9
    and children **134**.10, 12; **165**.22
    cigarettes
        and children **145**.2
        EU ban **145**.7
    and drinking behaviour, young people **143**.17, 19, 20
    junk food **88**.10, 11, 19, 20, 35, 37
    online **158**.5
    radio **158**.6
    regulation **134**.7,10
    television **158**.5
adware **158**.34
aesthetic surgery *see* cosmetic surgery
affirmative action **154**.36
affluence *see* wealth
affluenza **134**.5
affordable housing **181**.36
    Government strategies **130**.16, 33
    in rural areas **181**.3
    shortage of **130**.8, 23; **181**.6, 29
African-Caribbean people **115**.5
    pupils, exclusion **115**.19
African communities in UK
    HIV prevention campaigns **164**.24-5
    late HIV diagnosis **164**.17
age
    and alcohol consumption **143**.2, 17, 29; **176**.3, 14

Volume numbers appear first (in bold) followed by page numbers; a change in volume number is preceded by a semi-colon.

Vol. **76** The Water Crisis
Vol. **78** Threatened Species
Vol. **81** Alternative Therapies
Vol. **88** Food and Nutrition
Vol. **89** Refugees
Vol. **97** Energy Matters
Vol. **99** Exploited Children
Vol. **100** Stress and Anxiety
Vol. **107** Work Issues
Vol. **116** Grief and Loss
Vol. **118** Focus on Sport
Vol. **119** Transport Trends
Vol. **121** The Censorship Debate
Vol. **124** Parenting Issues
Vol. **125** Understanding Depression
Vol. **127** Eating Disorders
Vol. **128** The Cannabis Issue
Vol. **129** Gambling Trends
Vol. **130** Homelessness
Vol. **133** Teen Pregnancy and Lone Parents
Vol. **134** Customers and Consumerism
Vol. **135** Coping with Disability
Vol. **136** Self-Harm

Vol. **138** A Genetically Modified Future?
Vol. **139** The Education Problem
Vol. **140** Vegetarian and Vegan Diets
Vol. **141** Mental Health
Vol. **142** Media Issues
Vol. **143** Problem Drinking
Vol. **144** The Cloning Debate
Vol. **145** Smoking Trends
Vol. **146** Sustainability and Environment
Vol. **147** The Terrorism Problem
Vol. **148** Religious Beliefs
Vol. **149** A Classless Society?
Vol. **150** Migration and Population
Vol. **151** Climate Change
Vol. **152** Euthanasia and the Right to Die
Vol. **153** Sexual Orientation and Society
Vol. **154** The Gender Gap
Vol. **155** Domestic Abuse
Vol. **156** Travel and Tourism
Vol. **157** The Problem of Globalisation
Vol. **158** The Internet Revolution
Vol. **159** An Ageing Population
Vol. **160** Poverty and Exclusion

Vol. **161** Waste Issues
Vol. **162** Staying Fit
Vol. **163** Drugs in the UK
Vol. **164** The AIDS Crisis
Vol. **165** Bullying Issues
Vol. **166** Marriage and Cohabitation
Vol. **167** Our Human Rights
Vol. **168** Privacy and Surveillance
Vol. **169** The Animal Rights Debate
Vol. **170** Body Image and Self-Esteem
Vol. **171** Abortion – Rights and Ethics
Vol. **172** Racial and Ethnic Discrimination
Vol. **173** Sexual Health
Vol. **174** Selling Sex
Vol. **175** Citizenship and Participation
Vol. **176** Health Issues for Young People
Vol. **177** Crime in the UK
Vol. **178** Reproductive Ethics
Vol. **179** Tackling Child Abuse
Vol. **180** Money and Finances
Vol. **181** The Housing Issue

and child labour 99.2
and child soldiers 99.29-30
of children and divorcing parents 124.33-4
of criminal responsibility 177.19
and drinking behaviour, young people 143.16
and effects of alcohol 143.7
employment and gender 154.29
and employment, young people 180.20
and fertility 178.4
of first drink 143.16, 21
of first sexual intercourse 133.1
of foetal viability 171.23-4, 29
of homeless people 130.10, 14
of immigrants 150.8
and IVF 178.1, 19-20
at marriage 166.4, 6
   and risk of divorce 166.28
and sale of tobacco 145.3
and self-esteem 170.16
of self-harmers 136.4, 20
of smokers 145.1
and social identity, by neighbourhood 149.23
and stress levels 100.13
and suicidal intent 136.26
and voter turnout 131.19
voting age lowering 131.28, 29, 30
age of consent 99.25-6; 133.1; 173.1, 8, 11; 176.21-2
age discrimination 159.4, 8-13
   young people 159.12
age ratings
   films 121.23-5, 29-30
   video games 121.32-3
ageing
   ageing process 159.1-2, 31-2
   attitude to 159.14-15
   benefits of exercise 159.33; 162.12
   and health 159.31-9
   effect of lifestyle 159.33, 34
ageing population
   global 150.33, 35; 159.5, 6
   UK 150.28, 29, 39; 159.3
ageism see age discrimination
ageist bullying 165.9
agriculture
   and animal welfare 169.11-13
   and bioenergy 97.18
   and child labour 99.1, 2, 4; 167.32
   coffee growers 157.32, 33
   cotton farming 157.34
   egg production 140.38-9
   exotic animals 140.30
   fairtrade see fair trade
   and food nutrition 88.31-4
   and forests 146.30
   free trade in agriculture 88.33
   and global water shortages 76.3, 4, 8
   greenhouse gas production 151.7
   land use 146.25
   and migrant workers 150.11
   organic 146.25
   sustainable 146.27
   and water management 76.18, 36
   and water pollution 76.11
   see also animal welfare; food production; genetically modified (GM) crops; organic farming
agri-environment schemes 146.25
agro-chemicals 138.4
aid 160.34-9
   aid tying 157.10
   attitudes to 160.35-6, 37
   negative effects 160.38-9
   UK spending on aid 157.9-10
AIDS (Acquired Immune Deficiency Syndrome) 96.7, 17-22, 36-9; 164.1, 2
   AIDS-related illnesses 164.2
   anti-AIDS campaigns 164.23-5
   and assisted suicide 152.31
   and child labour 99.3
   and child soldiers 99.31
   'cures' 164.37-8
   deaths from 96.36
   and dementia 141.7
   and drug abuse 163.11
   education programmes 96.32
   global funding 96.39
   global statistics 96.17-18, 24, 30, 36, 38
   older people as carers 159.5
   orphans 96.39; 164.6, 7
   pandemic 96.31
   and parents of lesbians and gay people 153.9
   and the sexual exploitation of children 99.24
   tackling stigma and discrimination 96.19, 39
   treatments 96.18, 20
      antiretroviral therapy (ART) 96.36, 37, 38, 39; 164.2-3, 8-9, 29, 30-32
      fixed dose combinations (FDCs) 96.37
      vaccines 96.33-4; 34-5, 36
   UK statistics 96.20-2
   and young people 96.24-6, 29
   see also HIV (Human Immunodeficiency Virus)
air pollution 146.35-6
   monitoring 146.37
   and transport 119.1, 15, 16, 31
air travel
   airport security and congestion 156.1
   carbon dioxide emissions from 97.25
   and carbon offsetting 151.22, 33, 39
   disabled people 135.9
   effects of 156.21
   environmental impact 156.21, 26
   and pollution 119.16
   security 147.32
   and UK travel trends 156.3; 161.32
al-Qaida 147.7
alcohol 88.7, 24
   and accidents 176.15
   advertising, effects on young people 143.17, 19, 20
   alcopops 143.1, 3
   beer 143.1
   binge drinking see binge drinking
   and brain function 125.37; 143.4
   calories in 143.2

consumption
  children **143**.20
  older people **143**.9-10, 30
  regional variations **143**.13
  worldwide increase **143**.5
  young people **143**.2, 5, 15, 20, 37
daily benchmarks **143**.8, 25, 26-7, 34
  awareness of **143**.11, 34
deaths related to **143**.3, 6, 37; **163**.11
and depression **125**.2, 3, 36-7
and domestic violence **155**.4
drinks industry and responsible drinking **143**.27
and drugs **143**.3, 10
effects of **125**.37; **143**.3, 7, 23; **176**.4, 5, 15
health benefits of **143**.4, 7, 27
health risks of **143**.6, 9-10
and the law **143**.2-3
  young people **143**.2, 17
  see also drink-driving
licences **143**.2
and life expectancy **143**.13
and mental health **141**.34
and pregnancy **143**.3, 25, 27, 33-4
purchasing **143**.11
  underage **143**.16, 17, 20, 28
responsible drinking **143**.26-7, 29
risks
  of alcohol consumption **143**.3, 21-2
  of binge drinking **143**.4, 15
  in pregnancy **143**.3, 33
as self-medication for mental health problems **125**.36-7
and sex **173**.15
spirits **143**.1
strength **143**.1, 10
and stress **100**.27, 31, 37, 39
support groups **143**.38, 39
and television **143**.18-19, 20
trends **143**.1-24
UK legislation on the sale of **143**.2
underage drinking **125**.9; **143**.16, 20, 28; **176**.17-18
  see also young people and alcohol
units of **143**.1, 26; **176**.15

awareness of **143**.11
  drink labelling **143**.30, 32
wine
  health benefits **143**.4
  strength **143**.1
see also binge drinking; young people and alcohol
alcohol abuse **143**.25-39
  costs of **143**.36
  government strategies **143**.36-7
  and homeless people **130**.11, 12, 20
  and older people **143**.9-10, 30
  risks **143**.3, 4, 9, 13, 14
  signs of **143**.25, 35
  statistics **143**.37
  street drinking **130**.12
  treatment **143**.35, 38-9
  young people **143**.29, 37
  see also underage drinking
alcolocks **119**.8-9
alcopops **143**.1, 3
algae biofuels **151**.24-5
allergens, definition of **138**.4
alternative burials **116**.36, 38
alternative tourism **156**.24
aluminium recycling **161**.22, 27
Alzheimer's disease **141**.6; **159**.4, 36-9
  and animal experimentation **144**.34
  diagnosis using eye test **141**.19
  and diet **125**.12
amino acids **140**.7, 23
amnesia **141**.11
amphetamines **163**.4-5, 25
amphibians
  and evolution **78**.1
  and the exotic pet trade **78**.21
anabolic agents/steroids
  and the law **118**.35, 36
anaesthesia, and animal experiments **169**.17
anger
  and bereavement **116**.4, 8, 19
  dealing with **136**.3
  and domestic violence **155**.4, 34

Volume numbers appear first (in bold) followed by page numbers; a change in volume number is preceded by a semi-colon.

Vol. 76 The Water Crisis
Vol. 78 Threatened Species
Vol. 81 Alternative Therapies
Vol. 88 Food and Nutrition
Vol. 89 Refugees
Vol. 97 Energy Matters
Vol. 99 Exploited Children
Vol. 100 Stress and Anxiety
Vol. 107 Work Issues
Vol. 116 Grief and Loss
Vol. 118 Focus on Sport
Vol. 119 Transport Trends
Vol. 121 The Censorship Debate
Vol. 124 Parenting Issues
Vol. 125 Understanding Depression
Vol. 127 Eating Disorders
Vol. 128 The Cannabis Issue
Vol. 129 Gambling Trends
Vol. 130 Homelessness
Vol. 133 Teen Pregnancy and Lone Parents
Vol. 134 Customers and Consumerism
Vol. 135 Coping with Disability
Vol. 136 Self-Harm

Vol. 138 A Genetically Modified Future?
Vol. 139 The Education Problem
Vol. 140 Vegetarian and Vegan Diets
Vol. 141 Mental Health
Vol. 142 Media Issues
Vol. 143 Problem Drinking
Vol. 144 The Cloning Debate
Vol. 145 Smoking Trends
Vol. 146 Sustainability and Environment
Vol. 147 The Terrorism Problem
Vol. 148 Religious Beliefs
Vol. 149 A Classless Society?
Vol. 150 Migration and Population
Vol. 151 Climate Change
Vol. 152 Euthanasia and the Right to Die
Vol. 153 Sexual Orientation and Society
Vol. 154 The Gender Gap
Vol. 155 Domestic Abuse
Vol. 156 Travel and Tourism
Vol. 157 The Problem of Globalisation
Vol. 158 The Internet Revolution
Vol. 159 An Ageing Population
Vol. 160 Poverty and Exclusion

Vol. 161 Waste Issues
Vol. 162 Staying Fit
Vol. 163 Drugs in the UK
Vol. 164 The AIDS Crisis
Vol. 165 Bullying Issues
Vol. 166 Marriage and Cohabitation
Vol. 167 Our Human Rights
Vol. 168 Privacy and Surveillance
Vol. 169 The Animal Rights Debate
Vol. 170 Body Image and Self-Esteem
Vol. 171 Abortion – Rights and Ethics
Vol. 172 Racial and Ethnic Discrimination
Vol. 173 Sexual Health
Vol. 174 Selling Sex
Vol. 175 Citizenship and Participation
Vol. 176 Health Issues for Young People
Vol. 177 Crime in the UK
Vol. 178 Reproductive Ethics
Vol. 179 Tackling Child Abuse
Vol. 180 Money and Finances
Vol. 181 The Housing Issue

and traumatic bereavement 116.11
anger management and domestic abuse 155.34
animal cloning 144.30-39
    Dolly the sheep 144.1, 15, 30-31, 32, 34, 39
    and factory farming 144.35
    and food production 144.36-9
    and milk production 144.36-8, 39
    risks 144.39
animal experiments 169.14-26
    alternatives to 169.19, 21, 23
    arguments against 169.15-16, 19; 144.34
    arguments for 169.14-15, 18, 19, 22
    and genetically modified animals 144.34; 169.16, 17
    and humanism 140.32-3
    and non-toxological procedures 169.17
    public attitudes to 147.20
    regulation of 169.14, 20, 22
    statistics 169.17
    and toxicological procedures 169.17
    types of animals used 169.14, 17
animal feed 88.35-6
    GM content 138.25, 26
animal-human embryos 144.9, 11, 13, 14, 20
animal rights 169.1-3
animal rights activists
    and animal experiments 169.20
    terrorism 147.20-25
animal sentience 140.27-8; 169.2-3
animal suffering 140.32
    and animal experiments 169.14-15, 16, 25
    emotional suffering 169.2
    fur farming 169.5
    intensively farmed chickens 169.13
    and live transport 169.10
animal welfare 88.32-3, 35-6; 140.27-39; 169.1-13
    and animal experiments 169.20, 21, 25
    areas of concern 169.4
    consumer attitudes 140.14, 31, 33
    egg production 140.38-9
    the Five Freedoms 169.12
    Freedom Food mark 140.34
    and fur trade 169.6
    and humanism 140.31-3
    measuring 169.4
    meat production 140.13; 169.10, 13
    organic farms 140.35-6
    UK legislation on 121.7; 169.3, 4
anniversaries and grief 116.20
annual percentage rate (APR) 180.26
anorexia nervosa 127.1, 11-12
    as auto-immune disease 127.12
    children and young people 127.20
anthropomorphism 169.3
anti-bullying strategies
    cyberbullying 165.25-6
    peer mentoring 165.18
    schools 165.1, 8, 25
    workplaces 165.36, 38
anti-consumerism 146.39
anti-depressant drugs 125.24-5, 32
    and adolescents 125.8, 27

and children 125.27
and postnatal depression 125.18
and seasonal affective disorder 125.38
see also drug treatments for depression
anti-doping initiatives 118.25-8
    international 118.27-8, 31-2
    UK 118.26-7, 28, 30
anti-gay taunts, football 118.17
anti-psychotic drugs 125.19
anti-racism
    and football 118.14
    laws see legislation and racism
anti-retroviral therapy (ART) 96.36, 37, 38, 39; 164.2-3, 8-9, 29, 30-32
    during pregnancy 164.29-30, 31
    worldwide access to 164.39
anti-social behaviour 177.8
    and homelessness 130.7
Anti-Social Behaviour Orders (ASBOs) 177.8, 18, 25, 36-7
anti-terrorism measures
    legislation 147.2, 3, 27, 35-6
    Muslims' views on 115.34
    public attitudes to 167.24
antibiotics 88.14
    and organic farming 140.35
    resistance to 138.4
        and genetically modified organisms 138.13
antiretroviral therapy (ART) 96.36, 37, 38, 39
anxiety
    and childhood depression 125.28
    dangers of severe 100.21
    defining 100.21
    and depression 100.24
    and stress 100.2, 21
    symptoms of 100.21
appearance, effects of smoking 145.30-31
appetite-suppressing hormones 127.38-9
Applied AS awards 139.18
apprenticeships 107.36
aquifers, and global water supplies 76.7, 16, 19
armed conflict
    and the sexual exploitation of children 99.20-1
    war-affected children 99.32-3
    see also child soldiers
armed forces
    homeless ex-servicemen 130.11
    suicide of soldiers, Japan 136.39
aromatherapy 81.23, 36
    and cancer 81.10, 33
    and multiple sclerosis 81.30
    questions and answers 81.10
    and scientists 81.28, 29
    and stress relief 100.37
arranged marriages 166.16
arrests
    for drug use 128.11
    your rights 128.35-6; 177.35-6
artificial wombs 178.1-2
arts therapies 141.38
AS-levels (Advanced Supplementary levels) 139.4, 18
ASBOs (Anti-Social Behaviour Orders) 177.8, 18, 25, 36-7

Asian people
 British identity 115.37
 footballers 118.13, 15-16
Asperger's syndrome 135.34
aspirations gap 107.2
assault, equal protection for children 167.36-9; 179.31-2
assertiveness 170.10
assertiveness training and stress 100.32
Assisted Dying bill 152.16, 17, 33
 and disability rights 135.24
assisted reproductive technologies (ART) 178.11-12
 ethical concerns 178.11-12
 health problems for twins 178.21-2
 see also in vitro fertilisation
assisted suicide 152.1, 3, 5, 8-9
 arguments against 152.20-21
 arguments for 152.20
 and disabled people 135.24; 20-21
 and palliative care 152.22
 physician-assisted suicide 152.5, 7-8, 29-30, 31
asthma
 increasing 119.13, 26, 31
 and passive smoking 145.28, 29
asylum seekers 150.23
 conditions for granting refugee status 89.1
 dawn raids 167.27
 fleeing from conflict 89.7-8
 and HIV 96.39
  and homelessness 130.11-12, 19
 numbers of 89.2, 5, 6, 10
 top asylum nationalities 89.1-2, 5, 6, 10
 top countries receiving 89.2, 5, 10
 see also refugees
attempted suicide 136.27-8
 and gender 136.33
 and stress in young people 100.4
attendance centre orders 177.17, 26
attention deficit disorder (ADD) 127.7
 and eating disorders 127.10
attention deficit and hyperactivity disorder (ADHD) 141.19; 176.30
 and eating disorders 127.10

attention-seeking and self-harm 136.2-3, 8
authoritarian parenting style 124.8
authoritative parenting style 124.8
autism 135.34
auto-immune disease, anorexia as 127.12
autonomy 152.6
 effect of legalising euthanasia 152.6
 loss of, disabled people 152.20
 and right to die 152.3
aviation security 147.32

B

babies
 and euthanasia debate 152.4, 32, 33, 34
 and HIV 96.31, 39
 and mother's smoking 145.32-3
backstreet abortions 171.6, 22-3
bacteria 88.27, 28-9
 transgenic 144.11
bacterial vaginosis (BV) 173.17
baculoviruses 138.13-14
bail 177.37
balanced diet *see* healthy eating
banks 180.25-7
 banking crisis 180.4
 borrowing from 180.26-7
 opening an account 180.25
 and personal information 168.8
baptisms 148.22
bariatric (weight loss) surgery 162.3, 20
BASF GM potato trials 138.27-8
batteries, recycling 161.23, 28
battery eggs
 supermarket bans 140.38
begging 130.12
 children as beggars 99.3, 4
 giving to beggars 130.32
behaviour
 and poor body image 170.19
 effects of cannabis use 128.16

Volume numbers appear first (in bold) followed by page numbers; a change in volume number is preceded by a semi-colon.

Vol. 76 The Water Crisis
Vol. 78 Threatened Species
Vol. 81 Alternative Therapies
Vol. 88 Food and Nutrition
Vol. 89 Refugees
Vol. 97 Energy Matters
Vol. 99 Exploited Children
Vol. 100 Stress and Anxiety
Vol. 107 Work Issues
Vol. 116 Grief and Loss
Vol. 118 Focus on Sport
Vol. 119 Transport Trends
Vol. 121 The Censorship Debate
Vol. 124 Parenting Issues
Vol. 125 Understanding Depression
Vol. 127 Eating Disorders
Vol. 128 The Cannabis Issue
Vol. 129 Gambling Trends
Vol. 130 Homelessness
Vol. 133 Teen Pregnancy and Lone Parents
Vol. 134 Customers and Consumerism
Vol. 135 Coping with Disability
Vol. 136 Self-Harm

Vol. 138 A Genetically Modified Future?
Vol. 139 The Education Problem
Vol. 140 Vegetarian and Vegan Diets
Vol. 141 Mental Health
Vol. 142 Media Issues
Vol. 143 Problem Drinking
Vol. 144 The Cloning Debate
Vol. 145 Smoking Trends
Vol. 146 Sustainability and Environment
Vol. 147 The Terrorism Problem
Vol. 148 Religious Beliefs
Vol. 149 A Classless Society?
Vol. 150 Migration and Population
Vol. 151 Climate Change
Vol. 152 Euthanasia and the Right to Die
Vol. 153 Sexual Orientation and Society
Vol. 154 The Gender Gap
Vol. 155 Domestic Abuse
Vol. 156 Travel and Tourism
Vol. 157 The Problem of Globalisation
Vol. 158 The Internet Revolution
Vol. 159 An Ageing Population
Vol. 160 Poverty and Exclusion

Vol. 161 Waste Issues
Vol. 162 Staying Fit
Vol. 163 Drugs in the UK
Vol. 164 The AIDS Crisis
Vol. 165 Bullying Issues
Vol. 166 Marriage and Cohabitation
Vol. 167 Our Human Rights
Vol. 168 Privacy and Surveillance
Vol. 169 The Animal Rights Debate
Vol. 170 Body Image and Self-Esteem
Vol. 171 Abortion – Rights and Ethics
Vol. 172 Racial and Ethnic Discrimination
Vol. 173 Sexual Health
Vol. 174 Selling Sex
Vol. 175 Citizenship and Participation
Vol. 176 Health Issues for Young People
Vol. 177 Crime in the UK
Vol. 178 Reproductive Ethics
Vol. 179 Tackling Child Abuse
Vol. 180 Money and Finances
Vol. 181 The Housing Issue

children, effect of poverty 160.13
    gender differences 154.1, 9
    stress and behavioural changes 100.33
benefits *see* state benefits
benzene emissions 119.15; 146.36
bereavement 116.1-18
    children *see* children and bereavement
    counselling 116.6
    feelings 116.1, 3-4, 5, 7-9, 10-11, 19, 21-2, 30
    help from GP 116.2
    by murder 116.8
    and stress in young people 100.2
    by suicide 116.8
    support 116.2, 14-15
beta-blockers 118.37
betting 129.2
    see also gambling
bias and the media 142.10
bigorexia 127.19
bill payments and budgeting 180.30-31
Bills (parliamentary) 131.24
binding over 177.18
binge buying 134.13, 14
binge drinking 143.4, 13, 14
    children 143.20
    effects 176.15
    older people 143.9-10, 30
    parents' worries about 124.17
    risks 143.4, 14
    young people 143.5, 15; 176.14-16
binge eating 127.2, 15-16
binoculars, recycling 161.23
biodegradability of litter 161.16
biodiesel vehicles 119.21
biodiversity 146.18-21, 33
    and climate change 151.9
    and endangered animals 78.6
    framework for measuring 78.27
    loss of freshwater 76.35
    protecting 146.20-21
    threats to 146.19, 21
    value of 146.18-19
bioenergy 97.18
    biofuels 97.9; 138.4; 146.39; 151.24-5
    biomass 97.5, 6, 9, 11, 18
biological effects of compulsive gambling 129.29
biological attacks, response to 147.31
biological parents and parental responsibility 153.33
biological resources 146.9
    see also biodiversity
biology
    and gender development 154.1
    and sexual orientation 153.6, 7
biometrics
    biometric fingerprinting in schools 168.30
    biometric travel documents 168.13
    problems with 168.18
biotechnology
    definition 138.4
    public attitudes to 138.15-16; 144.19
bipolar affective disorder (manic depression) 125.2, 4, 10,

    19-20; 141.14-15
    defining 125.19
    experiences of sufferers 141.28-9
    symptoms 125.19
    treatments 125.19-20
birth control *see* contraception
birth country, non-white ethnic groups 115.38
    UK as birth country 131.8
birth rates
    births outside marriage 124.22
    to foreign parents in UK 150.29, 30
    to teenage mothers 133.2
    see also teenage pregnancies
bisexuality 153.10-12
    definition 153.1
    discrimination 153.2
black people
    church membership 148.23
    educational performance of children 115.19-20
    pupils 115.18-21; 139.9
    see also employment and racism; ethnic minorities; racism
bladder repair, stem cell therapy 144.21
blame, feelings of, following bereavement 116.8, 11, 19
blasphemy laws 121.16
    and cartoons of Mohammed 121.12
blogs 142.37; 158.3, 8
blood donation and HIV 164.1
blood doping 118.38
blood pressure *see* high blood pressure (hypertension)
blood products and HIV 96.14; 164.1, 19-20, 25
blood sports 169.27-39
blood sugar levels 88.15
    and binge eating 127.15
blood tests
    for HIV diagnosis 164.2, 20-21
    for mental illness diagnosis 141.18
blue badge scheme (disabled people) 135.7-8
BMI *see* body mass index
boardroom positions, women 154.34
bodily privacy 168.2
body dysmorphic disorder/dysmorphophobia 127.18-19;
    170.29-30
body image 170.17-39
    and bullying 165.8-9
    children 170.21-2, 24
    definition 170.17
    and eating disorders 127.27
    and exercise 141.39; 176.7
    girls, and sport 170.39
    improving 170.17, 20, 37-8
    and the media 127.23, 25-6, 27; 170.22, 23, 24, 28, 30-31, 38
    negative 170.17, 19-20
    positive 170.17, 37
    and self-esteem 170.19
    study 127.29
    and video games 170.27
body mass index (BMI) 88.8; 127.32; 162.1, 4, 23
    and children 127.36; 162.1
    criticism of 162.5
body shapes 127.22
    effect of smoking 145.31

body weight **88**.1, 12, 18
  and body image **170**.19, 38
  and fertility **178**.5
  and smoking **145**.30-31
  see also obesity; weight management
bonded labour **167**.20, 32
bone density, effects of eating disorders **127**.5
bone marrow stem cells
  and heart disease treatment **144**.23
  and sperm cell creation **144**.29
bone marrow transplants **144**.24
  saviour siblings **178**.28-9
books
  children's books and gay issues **153**.19-20
  and portrayal of disabled children **135**.21
border controls **89**.20; **147**.29
borrowing
  from banks **180**.26-7
  see also debt
boys and young men
  attitudes to sex **173**.12-13
  and child labour **99**.2
  child soldiers **99**.31, 36
  and education **154**.22-6
    foundation stage **154**.23
    raising educational achievement **154**.25
    single-sex teaching **154**.26
    subject choices **154**.22, 26
    underachievement **154**.23
  and mental health problems **141**.1
  and parenthood **133**.25-7
  and puberty **127**.22
  self-harm **136**.7
  sexual exploitation of **99**.16, 21
  and smoking **145**.2, 5
  street children **99**.19
brain
  effects of alcohol on **125**.37; **143**.4
  effects of cannabis on **128**.34
  effect of diet **141**.30-31
  effect of nicotine **145**.25, 26
  research, use of primates **169**.24-6

stem cell therapy for brain damage **144**.22
brand awareness, children **134**.11
brand image and advertising **134**.8-9
brand names
  and bullying **165**.22
  as children's names **134**.12
breakfast, importance of **127**.23
breast cancer
  and complementary therapies **81**.23
  and abortions **171**.3
breast surgery, teenagers **170**.32-3
Britain, asylum seekers
  appeals process **89**.13-14, 29, 33
  asylum claims procedure **89**.12, 13-14
  asylum legislation **89**.11, 12, 33, 39
  citizenship acceptance **89**.37
  costs of the asylum system **89**.11, 30
  detention centres **89**.12, 13
  health treatment **89**.19-20
  legal aid **89**.29
  number of asylum claims **89**.16, 18, 23; **150**.4, 23
  refused asylum applications **89**.11, 13-14, 18
  welfare support **89**.12, 13, 14, 19, 30, 38
British history, importance of teaching **131**.7
British identity **131**.1-14; **156**.11
  Asians **115**.37
  and non-white ethnic groups **115**.38
  see also Britishness
British mentality and class **149**.6
British population
  ethnic groups **115**.3
  mixed-race relationships **115**.24
British tourists
  behaviour **156**.31
  visits abroad **156**.4
Britishness **131**.1-14
  decline of **131**.9
  effect of devolution **131**.5, 6
  and Islamophobia **131**.11
  and multiculturalism **131**.10
  see also British identity
broadband services **158**.5-6, 17

Volume numbers appear first (in bold) followed by page numbers; a change in volume number is preceded by a semi-colon.

Vol. 76 The Water Crisis
Vol. 78 Threatened Species
Vol. 81 Alternative Therapies
Vol. 88 Food and Nutrition
Vol. 89 Refugees
Vol. 97 Energy Matters
Vol. 99 Exploited Children
Vol. 100 Stress and Anxiety
Vol. 107 Work Issues
Vol. 116 Grief and Loss
Vol. 118 Focus on Sport
Vol. 119 Transport Trends
Vol. 121 The Censorship Debate
Vol. 124 Parenting Issues
Vol. 125 Understanding Depression
Vol. 127 Eating Disorders
Vol. 128 The Cannabis Issue
Vol. 129 Gambling Trends
Vol. 130 Homelessness
Vol. 133 Teen Pregnancy and Lone Parents
Vol. 134 Customers and Consumerism
Vol. 135 Coping with Disability
Vol. 136 Self-Harm

Vol. 138 A Genetically Modified Future?
Vol. 139 The Education Problem
Vol. 140 Vegetarian and Vegan Diets
Vol. 141 Mental Health
Vol. 142 Media Issues
Vol. 143 Problem Drinking
Vol. 144 The Cloning Debate
Vol. 145 Smoking Trends
Vol. 146 Sustainability and Environment
Vol. 147 The Terrorism Problem
Vol. 148 Religious Beliefs
Vol. 149 A Classless Society?
Vol. 150 Migration and Population
Vol. 151 Climate Change
Vol. 152 Euthanasia and the Right to Die
Vol. 153 Sexual Orientation and Society
Vol. 154 The Gender Gap
Vol. 155 Domestic Abuse
Vol. 156 Travel and Tourism
Vol. 157 The Problem of Globalisation
Vol. 158 The Internet Revolution
Vol. 159 An Ageing Population
Vol. 160 Poverty and Exclusion

Vol. 161 Waste Issues
Vol. 162 Staying Fit
Vol. 163 Drugs in the UK
Vol. 164 The AIDS Crisis
Vol. 165 Bullying Issues
Vol. 166 Marriage and Cohabitation
Vol. 167 Our Human Rights
Vol. 168 Privacy and Surveillance
Vol. 169 The Animal Rights Debate
Vol. 170 Body Image and Self-Esteem
Vol. 171 Abortion – Rights and Ethics
Vol. 172 Racial and Ethnic Discrimination
Vol. 173 Sexual Health
Vol. 174 Selling Sex
Vol. 175 Citizenship and Participation
Vol. 176 Health Issues for Young People
Vol. 177 Crime in the UK
Vol. 178 Reproductive Ethics
Vol. 179 Tackling Child Abuse
Vol. 180 Money and Finances
Vol. 181 The Housing Issue

for low-income families **158**.18
broadcasting
    illegal **142**.7
    mergers **142**.4
    see also radio; television
broadcasting regulation **121**.36-7
broadsheet newspapers **142**.8
brownfield sites **181**.36
BSE (bovine spongiform encephalopathy)
    and freedom of information **88**.14
Bt cotton **138**.35
BTecs, impact of specialist diplomas **139**.23-4
Buddhism **148**.2
    festivals **148**.2
    food rules **148**.11
Budget, the **180**.24
budgeting **180**.30-31
    for home buying **181**.24
building industry *see* construction industry
building societies **180**.25-7
building waste recycling **161**.23
building your own home **181**.30-31
bulimia nervosa **127**.1-2, 13-14
    children and young people **127**.20
bullfighting **169**.37-9
bullies
    characteristics of **165**.20, 21
    consequences for **165**.19, 26
    risk of suicide **165**.21-2
bullying **165**.1-39
    causes **165**.5
    cyber-bullying **165**.2, 9, 23-31, 37-9
    definitions **165**.1, 3-5
    effects **165**.1, 19
    fears of gay parents **153**.22
    forms of **165**.3-5, 6, 8-9, 19
    gender differences **154**.25
    homophobic **153**.14-18; **165**.2, 9, 12-14
    how to help **165**.6
    in the community **165**.7-8
    prevalence of **165**.1-2, 18
    reasons for **165**.1, 5, 18
    risk factors **165**.3
    statistics **165**.1-2
    and stress in young people **100**.1, 2, 4
    and suicide **165**.20, 21-2
    at work *see* workplace bullying
    and workplace stress **100**.14, 15
    see also bullies; racist bullying; school bullying; workplace
      bullying
burial **116**.37-9
    alternative burials **116**.36, 38
    natural **134**.31
    on private land **116**.39
    at sea **116**.39
burns, first aid **136**.23
burying bad news **121**.17-18
bus travel
    and disabled people **135**.8-9
    and pollution **119**.12
    trends **119**.1

businesses
    anti-terrorism measures **147**.32
    and biodiversity protection **146**.20
    and environmentalism **146**.38-9
    sustainable **146**.7
butadiene **146**.36
buying a home
    costs **181**.24
    young people **181**.26

C

Cabinet, The **131**.21
caffeine **118**.35
    and mental health **141**.35
calcium **88**.6
    dietary sources **140**.4; **176**.8
    teenagers' requirements **176**.8
    and vegetarian diets **140**.3
calorie content of alcohol **143**.2
calorie intake **88**.1, 12; **162**.8
    teenagers **176**.8
campaigns and the media **142**.10
campylobacter **88**.28
cancer
    and cannabis use **128**.17, 19, 28
    and complementary therapies **81**.3, 10, 21, 27, 32-3
    leukaemia, stem cell therapy **144**.21
    lung cancer **145**.34
    and passive smoking **145**.2, 29
    prevention **88**.17, 30
    skin **176**.10-11
    and smoking **145**.34
    stem cell therapy for blood cancers **144**.21
    and vegetarian diets **140**.9, 11
    see also breast cancer; cervical cancer; lung cancer
cancer salves (escharotics) **81**.33
cancer treatments
    and genetically modified hens **138**.20-21
cannabinoids **118**.38
    and multiple sclerosis **128**.36
    THC **128**.3, 34
cannabis **163**.6
    appearance **128**.1
    cannabis cafés 27-8
    cannabis oil **128**.4, 6, 23
    cannabis resin (hashish) **128**.1, 3, 6, 23
      seizures of **128**.31
    chemical content **128**.13-14
    children's use **128**.16
      and depression **128**.14
    classification **128**.13
    compulsive use **128**.15
    cultivation **128**.23-4; 33-4; **163**.25
      penalties for **128**.31
      skunk **128**.3-4
    dealing, penalties for **128**.2, 9, 13
    dependence on **128**.2, 8, 15
    and driving **128**.14
    eating **128**.5

effects of **163**.6, 35-6
  desired **128**.4, 14
  harmful **128**.1-2, 4-5, 8-9, 13-15, 28
  on the brain **128**.34
  on learning and educational performance **128**.14
  medicinal **128**.4, 28, 36, 37
  skunk **128**.2
forms of **128**.1, 3-4, 6, 13
giving up **128**.2, 10
and hard drug use **128**.9-10, 11, 28
herbal cannabis (marijuana/grass) **128**.2,3,6, 23
  seizures of **128**.31
history **128**.7
home cultivation of **128**.3-4, 30-31
and the law **128**.2, 7, 9, 26-38
legalisation debate **128**.7
market **128**.23-4
medicinal use of **128**.4, 28, 36, 37
  and the law **128**.37
  and multiple sclerosis **81**.30, 31; **128**.36, 37
and mental health **128**.5, 8, 14-15; **163**.35
and multiple sclerosis **81**.30, 31; **128**.36, 37
names for **128**.1
penalties
  for cultivation **128**.31
  for possession **128**.2, 9, 13, 27, 30, 31, 32
  for supply **128**.2, 9, 13
potency of **128**.6
  resin **128**.3
  skunk **128**.2
prices **128**.2, 6
production *see* cannabis cultivation
psychosis **128**.15
purity **128**.1, 2
reclassification of **128**.13, 26-8, 29; **163**.32, 35-6
  criticized **128**.38
  effect on health **128**.30-32, 38
  public attitudes to **128**.12
and respiratory health **128**.18-19
seizures of **128**.23, 31
smoking **128**.8
  effects of **128**.5, 18-19

sources **128**.3, 34
THC (delta-9 tetrahydrocannabinol)**128**.3, 34
use
  giving up **128**.2, 10
  methods of use **128**.5, 6, 13
  prevalence **128**.6, 21, 22
  public attitudes to **128**.12
  users, children **128**.16
cans, recycling **161**.27
canvassers **131**.18
capital flight **157**.5
car batteries, recycling **161**.28
carbohydrates **88**.2, 5-6, 15
carbon
  carbon credits **151**.36-7
  low carbon technologies **97**.4
carbon dioxide
  atmospheric concentration **151**.7
  CO_2 equivalent **151**.13
  sources of **151**.4
carbon dioxide emissions
  agriculture **151**.7
  and air transport **97**.25
  and biomass **97**.18
  from fossil fuel burning **97**.1, 4
  from power stations **97**.3
  and global warming **151**.3
  public awareness of **97**.34
  reducing **97**.2; **151**.2, 13
  from tourism **156**.25
  from transport **119**.14, 15, 16, 24, 30
    in the UK **97**.5, 21
  see also greenhouse gas
carbon monoxide **146**.36
  transport emissions **119**.15
carbon offsetting **151**.20-22, 33-5; **156**.1
carbon sequestration **151**.26
carbon sinks **151**.26
carbon trading **151**.36-7
cardboard recycling **161**.24, 26-7
cardiology, stem cell therapy **144**.22, 23, 28
cardiovascular disease *see* heart disease

Volume numbers appear first (in bold) followed by page numbers; a change in volume number is preceded by a semi-colon.

Vol. 76 The Water Crisis
Vol. 78 Threatened Species
Vol. 81 Alternative Therapies
Vol. 88 Food and Nutrition
Vol. 89 Refugees
Vol. 97 Energy Matters
Vol. 99 Exploited Children
Vol. 100 Stress and Anxiety
Vol. 107 Work Issues
Vol. 116 Grief and Loss
Vol. 118 Focus on Sport
Vol. 119 Transport Trends
Vol. 121 The Censorship Debate
Vol. 124 Parenting Issues
Vol. 125 Understanding Depression
Vol. 127 Eating Disorders
Vol. 128 The Cannabis Issue
Vol. 129 Gambling Trends
Vol. 130 Homelessness
Vol. 133 Teen Pregnancy and Lone Parents
Vol. 134 Customers and Consumerism
Vol. 135 Coping with Disability
Vol. 136 Self-Harm

Vol. 138 A Genetically Modified Future?
Vol. 139 The Education Problem
Vol. 140 Vegetarian and Vegan Diets
Vol. 141 Mental Health
Vol. 142 Media Issues
Vol. 143 Problem Drinking
Vol. 144 The Cloning Debate
Vol. 145 Smoking Trends
Vol. 146 Sustainability and Environment
Vol. 147 The Terrorism Problem
Vol. 148 Religious Beliefs
Vol. 149 A Classless Society?
Vol. 150 Migration and Population
Vol. 151 Climate Change
Vol. 152 Euthanasia and the Right to Die
Vol. 153 Sexual Orientation and Society
Vol. 154 The Gender Gap
Vol. 155 Domestic Abuse
Vol. 156 Travel and Tourism
Vol. 157 The Problem of Globalisation
Vol. 158 The Internet Revolution
Vol. 159 An Ageing Population
Vol. 160 Poverty and Exclusion

Vol. 161 Waste Issues
Vol. 162 Staying Fit
Vol. 163 Drugs in the UK
Vol. 164 The AIDS Crisis
Vol. 165 Bullying Issues
Vol. 166 Marriage and Cohabitation
Vol. 167 Our Human Rights
Vol. 168 Privacy and Surveillance
Vol. 169 The Animal Rights Debate
Vol. 170 Body Image and Self-Esteem
Vol. 171 Abortion – Rights and Ethics
Vol. 172 Racial and Ethnic Discrimination
Vol. 173 Sexual Health
Vol. 174 Selling Sex
Vol. 175 Citizenship and Participation
Vol. 176 Health Issues for Young People
Vol. 177 Crime in the UK
Vol. 178 Reproductive Ethics
Vol. 179 Tackling Child Abuse
Vol. 180 Money and Finances
Vol. 181 The Housing Issue

care gap **135**.20
care homes **159**.27-8; **179**.10-11
care leavers and homelessness **130**.11, 14
care services for older people **159**.4
    concerns about **159**.28
    funding **159**.29
    rising costs **159**.26
career advice **107**.32
    gender bias **154**.28, 35
career breaks **107**.27
career progression **107**.28
carers
    and flexible working **107**.17-18
    older people as carers **159**.4, 5
    statistics **154**.30
    young carers **135**.10-12
carotenes **88**.2, 5
carrier bags *see* plastic bags
cars
    attitudes to car use **97**.35, 36
    batteries, recycling **161**.28
    car clubs **119**.33
    cleaner fuels **119**.20-23
    congestion *see* congestion, traffic
    dependency on **119**.7
    drink-driving *see* drink-driving
    emissions reduction **151**.39
    fuel efficient **119**.20-24
    ownership **119**.7, 11, 29
    recycling **161**.23
    reducing use of **119**.39
    sharing **119**.32-3
    speeding **119**.3, 4, 8
        and pedestrian injuries **119**.5, 30-31
        and speed cameras **119**.4, 17, 18
        speed limiters **119**.18
    spending on **134**.4, 25
    tax and fuel efficiency **119**.24
    usage trends **119**.1, 7-9, 11, 13, 29; **161**.31
    see also road accidents
cartilage repair using stem cells **144**.21
cartoons of Mohammed **121**.10-13, 15-16; **142**.34
cash cards **180**.13, 25
cash machine withdrawals **180**.16, 17
cash payments **180**.13
    statistics **180**.16-17
cashless society **180**.15-16
casinos **129**.2
    new, UK **129**.15, 34
    supercasino **129**.14-16, 34
casual sex, international comparisons **173**.6
catalogues and credit payment **134**.22
cathartic role of football **141**.32
Catholic Church
    and abortion **171**.17, 18
    and embryo research **178**.35
    and euthanasia **152**.11, 29
    and faith schools **148**.35
    and IVF **178**.17
    see also Christianity
cattle

cloning **144**.36-8
    and hybrid embryos **144**.11
    see also livestock farming
cautions **177**.36
CCTV (Closed Circuit Television) **168**.6, 7, 8-9, 22-5
    and anti-social behaviour **177**.8
    and crime prevention **168**.23-4
    in schools **168**.25
    and sound recording **168**.24
    statistics **168**.22
celebrities as parental role models **124**.6
celebrity culture
    and body image **170**.22
    and cosmetic surgery **170**.33
cell ageing **159**.1
cell nuclear replacement **144**.15
censorship **121**.1-2
    films **121**.22, 23-5
    and the Internet **121**.18-21; **158**.37
    television **121**.36-7
census **150**.36
    ethnic group questions **115**.3
    religious affiliation results **148**.6-7
cereals **88**.5-6, 15
cerebral palsy and learning disabilities **135**.34
certificates of identity **168**.13
cervical cancer
    screening **173**.39
    vaccination **173**.38-9
challenging racism **115**.2
    at work **115**.12
charitable giving **130**.32, 33
chatrooms
    and bullying **165**.24
    and sexual offences **158**.35
'chavs'
    children's perceptions of **149**.10-11
    prejudice against **149**.8
Chechen conflict and child soldiers **99**.37
cheese and vegetarian diets **140**.6, 18, 22, 26
chemical/biological incidents, response to **147**.31
chemicals, disposal **161**.23
cheques **180**.13, 25
chickens, intensively farmed **169**.13
child abuse **179**.1-12
    and dependency **141**.10
    and dissociative disorders **141**.12-13
    emotional **179**.1; 5
    getting help **179**.5-6, 7
    help for professionals **179**.11-12
    and mental health problems **141**.10, 12-13
    neglect **179**.3, 5
        reporting **179**.7
        taking children into care **179**.10-11
    online **179**.15-16, 17
    physical **179**.1-2, 5
        see also corporal punishment; smacking
    prevalence **179**.4, 8-9, 13, 15, 17
    signs and symptoms **179**.5-6
    see also corporal punishment; paedophiles; sexual abuse;
        smacking

child labour **99**.1-15; **167**.30-31, 32
  and age of child **99**.2
  attitudes to **99**.1
  combating **99**.11-13
  defining **99**.2, 3
  demand for **99**.3
  domestic work **99**.1, 4, 7-10
  economic benefits of eliminating **99**.1, 6, 15
  economic truths of **99**.14-15
  and education **99**.3, 7, 10, 11-12, 15
  and human rights **99**.4, 6
  impact on a child **99**.2, 3
  legislation and laws
    enforcement of **99**.11
    improving **99**.11
  organisations to take action against **99**.4
  and poverty **99**.2, 3, 4, 11, 12, 14-15
  reasons for **99**.1, 2-3, 3-4
  statistics **99**.1, 2, 14
  suitability for certain types of work **99**.4
  types of **99**.1, 2, 3, 4
child mortality, Milliennium Goals **160**.31
child pornography **99**.1, 16, 17, 20, 24, 25
  online **179**.17
child poverty **160**.2, 3, 11, 19, 25, 29
  public attitudes to **160**.14
  and education **160**.16-22
  and family debt **160**.12
  and women's poverty **160**.15
child prostitution **99**.1, 16, 17, 25-6, 27-8; **167**.32
child psychiatrists **100**.2
child safety concerns of parents **124**.13-14
child safety orders **177**.18
child sex tourism **156**.37-9
child slavery **167**.20, 32-3
child soldiers **99**.1, 4, 29-39; **167**.32, 33-4
  age of **99**.29-30
  benefits of ending child soldier use **99**.39
  defining **99**.29
  girls **99**.29, 31, 36
  harmful effects of being **99**.31, 36
  and human rights atrocities **99**.30

  and non-governmental armed groups **99**.30
  statistics **99**.29
  see also war-affected children
Child Support Agency **133**.34, 37
  problems **124**.35; **133**.30
child trafficking **167**.32, 34
childbirth
  deaths in **154**.12
  and exercise **162**.32
  see also post-natal depression
childcare
  advice **133**.37-8
  costs **124**.3
  emergency childcare **107**.22
  experience for teenagers **133**.27
  and fathers **124**.7-10, 11
  and flexible working **107**.12, 16, 21, 23
  and grandmothers **124**.37-8
  statistics **154**.30
childhood obesity **88**.3, 11; **127**.33, 36-7; **162**.6, 13-14, 25-9; **176**.2, 3
  effects of exercise **162**.28, 29
  measurement in schools **127**.36
  as neglect **162**.27
childhood problems
  and dependency **141**.9-10
  and post traumatic stress disorder **141**.3
childlessness for financial reasons **124**.18
ChildLine
  and domestic violence **155**.25
  and eating disorders **127**.20-21
  number of calls **181**.13
  and racism **115**.1
  and sex worries **173**.7
  and sexual abuse **179**.13-15
  and stepfamily worries **124**.23
  and suicide **176**.35, 36-7
children
  abuse *see* child abuse
  and advertising **134**.10, 12
  alcohol consumption **143**.20; **176**.3, 14
  alcohol and mental health problems **125**.9

Volume numbers appear first (in bold) followed by page numbers; a change in volume number is preceded by a semi-colon.

Vol. 76 The Water Crisis
Vol. 78 Threatened Species
Vol. 81 Alternative Therapies
Vol. 88 Food and Nutrition
Vol. 89 Refugees
Vol. 97 Energy Matters
Vol. 99 Exploited Children
Vol. 100 Stress and Anxiety
Vol. 107 Work Issues
Vol. 116 Grief and Loss
Vol. 118 Focus on Sport
Vol. 119 Transport Trends
Vol. 121 The Censorship Debate
Vol. 124 Parenting Issues
Vol. 125 Understanding Depression
Vol. 127 Eating Disorders
Vol. 128 The Cannabis Issue
Vol. 129 Gambling Trends
Vol. 130 Homelessness
Vol. 133 Teen Pregnancy and Lone Parents
Vol. 134 Customers and Consumerism
Vol. 135 Coping with Disability
Vol. 136 Self-Harm

Vol. 138 A Genetically Modified Future?
Vol. 139 The Education Problem
Vol. 140 Vegetarian and Vegan Diets
Vol. 141 Mental Health
Vol. 142 Media Issues
Vol. 143 Problem Drinking
Vol. 144 The Cloning Debate
Vol. 145 Smoking Trends
Vol. 146 Sustainability and Environment
Vol. 147 The Terrorism Problem
Vol. 148 Religious Beliefs
Vol. 149 A Classless Society?
Vol. 150 Migration and Population
Vol. 151 Climate Change
Vol. 152 Euthanasia and the Right to Die
Vol. 153 Sexual Orientation and Society
Vol. 154 The Gender Gap
Vol. 155 Domestic Abuse
Vol. 156 Travel and Tourism
Vol. 157 The Problem of Globalisation
Vol. 158 The Internet Revolution
Vol. 159 An Ageing Population
Vol. 160 Poverty and Exclusion

Vol. 161 Waste Issues
Vol. 162 Staying Fit
Vol. 163 Drugs in the UK
Vol. 164 The AIDS Crisis
Vol. 165 Bullying Issues
Vol. 166 Marriage and Cohabitation
Vol. 167 Our Human Rights
Vol. 168 Privacy and Surveillance
Vol. 169 The Animal Rights Debate
Vol. 170 Body Image and Self-Esteem
Vol. 171 Abortion – Rights and Ethics
Vol. 172 Racial and Ethnic Discrimination
Vol. 173 Sexual Health
Vol. 174 Selling Sex
Vol. 175 Citizenship and Participation
Vol. 176 Health Issues for Young People
Vol. 177 Crime in the UK
Vol. 178 Reproductive Ethics
Vol. 179 Tackling Child Abuse
Vol. 180 Money and Finances
Vol. 181 The Housing Issue

anti-extremism education **147**.34
attitudes to poverty **160**.4
and the beauty industry **170**.25-6
and bereavement **116**.1, 9, 19-28
  bereavement statistics **116**.20, 21
  bereavement support **116**.15, 28
body image concerns **170**.21-2, 24
books showing gay couples **153**.19-20
and bullying **165**.3-5
in care, educational disadvantages **160**.22
as carers **135**.10-12
and censorship
  films **121**.23-5
  video games **121**.32-3
  videos **121**.26
of cohabiting couples **124**.22; **166**.14-15
communication trends **158**.4
and consumerism **134**.11-12
contact with parents after divorce **166**.37-8
costs of raising **124**.3; **134**.25
cycling **119**.28, 30
death
  children's questions about **116**.26-7
  children's understanding of **116**.22
and depression **125**.27-8
in developing countries
  deaths and diseases from water-related illness **76**.2, 3,
    5, 9, 13, 14
  and global water supplies **76**.13-14
  and hygiene education **76**.14
  and sanitation provision **76**.13-14
  and water collection **76**.13, 19-20
developing responsibility **124**.13-14
disabled see disabled children
and divorce **124**.24, 29-30, 32-4; **166**.4-5, 29-31, 34-8
and domestic violence **155**.1, 4, 5, 19-25
drug awareness **163**.27
earning money **180**.20
and eating disorders **127**.3, 20-21
ethnic minorities, and education **115**.18, 19-21
exercise, lack of **162**.13, 15, 25
falling out with parents **124**.18
and fathers **124**.7-11
and food advertising **88**.10, 11, 20, 35, 37
and funerals **116**.23, 26
and gambling
  online gambling **129**.18
of gay couples **153**.20-22
gender development **154**.1
and grief **116**.19-28
health **176**.2-3
  government strategy **162**.17
    and transport **119**.13-14, 31
  healthy weight **162**.25
and HIV/AIDS **96**.20, 39; **164**.6-8
  preventing HIV transmission from mother **164**.25, 27,
    29-30, 31
and homelessness **130**.23
housing problems **181**.13, 14
inequality **167**.35
and the Internet **158**.20-21, 27-30

of lone parents **124**.33-4; **133**.28, 31
and media violence **121**.33, 34, 35
and the mediation process **166**.39
and mental health
  mental health problems **125**.16; **141**.1, 20-21
  mental health programmes **141**.37
  effect of parents' mental health problems **141**.24-5
obesity see childhood obesity
online gaming addiction **158**.39
online safety **165**.26-7, 30-31
and passive smoking **145**.2, 28-9
and parental relationships **166**.32
and parental separation **166**.4-5, 29, 30, 31, 32
and poverty see child poverty
and prison see youth custody
and racism **115**.1-2, 9
refugees **89**.39
and road accidents **119**.5, 28, 30-31
and road safety **119**.5-6
safety concerns of parents **124**.13-14
and self-esteem **170**.9-10
sex, worries about **173**.7
sex education **133**.15, 17
sexual abuse see sexual abuse
slavery **167**.20-32-3
smacking see smacking
and smoking **145**.2-3; **176**.3, 12-13
  attitudes to smoking **145**.20
  health effects **145**.2; **176**.12-13
  and the law **145**.3; **176**.13
  mother smoking in pregnancy **145**.32-3
  effects of nicotine **145**.27
  passive smoking **145**.2, 28-9
social differences, perceptions of **149**.9-12
and social housing **181**.9-11
and stepfamilies **124**.23-8
and suicide **176**.35, 36-7
of teenage mothers **133**.10
and television
  parental control of viewing **121**.26, 27, 34
and terrorism **147**.32
time spent with fathers **124**.7-8, 9, 11
travel to school **119**.26, 29-30
and video classification **121**.32-3
and video games **121**.32-3
and women's earnings **154**.35-6
children's rights **167**.28-39
  and corporal punishment **167**.36-8; **179**.30, 31-2
  statistics **167**.30
  UN Convention on the Rights of the Child **167**.28-9
chimeras (human-animal hybrids) **144**.10-12
  for stem cell research **178**.35
Chinese medicine **81**.2, 3
  and cancer **81**.33
  and endangered species **81**.15
  herbal medicine **81**.14-15, 39
  see also complementary medicine (CM)
chiropractic **81**.8-9, 23, 36
  effectiveness of **81**.24
  misdiagnosis and dangers of **81**.23, 24
  regulation of **81**.23

and scientists **81**.28, 29
chlamydia **173**.17, 20; **176**.25, 26
    online testing for **173**.28
chocolate **88**.18-19, 31
    vegan **140**.22, 26
choice as consumer right **134**.1
cholera **76**.2, 12, 13, 32
Christianity **148**.2
    and the Census (2001) **148**.6, 7
    and church attendance **148**.7, 18-19, 20-21, 23, 27
    degree of commitment **148**.7
    denominations **148**.6
    discrimination against **148**.28
    festivals **148**.2
    and food culture **148**.10
    funerals **116**.33
church attendance **148**.7, 18-19, 20-21, 23, 27
Church of England
    baptisms **148**.22
    and euthanasia **152**.34
    and faith schools **148**.35
    as state religion (established church) **148**.21-2
cider, strength of **143**.1
cigarettes
    chemicals in **145**.1
    cost **145**.3, 17
    pack size **145**.19
    sales, effect of smoking ban **145**.16-17
    see also smoking
circles of support, for sex offenders **179**.22-3
circus animals **169**.9-10
cities *see* cars, congestion; urban areas; urban growth
citizen photojournalism **142**.23
citizenship **89**.37
    British identity **131**.1-14
    European Union **131**.38
    global **131**.37
    government **131**.15-25
    survey **131**.2-3
    test **131**.12
    young people **131**.26-39
Citizenship Education in schools **131**.36

city colleges and special educational needs **135**.36
civic involvement, young people **131**.31-2
civil liberties
    and media regulation **142**.1-2
civil marriage ceremonies **166**.6
civil partnerships **153**.26-30
    dissolution **166**.21-2
    numbers **153**.29-30
    and parental responsibility **153**.33
civil protest **121**.14
civil rights on surveillance **168**.10
civil wars **89**.7-8
CJD (Creutzfeld Jacob disease) **141**.7
class *see* social class
class A drugs
    young people's use **163**.26-7
class sizes (schools) **139**.1, 12
classification
    of drugs **128**.26; **163**.2, 31, 33-4, 37
    of films **121**.22, 23-5, 29-30
    of video games **121**.32-3
cleaner fuels **119**.20-23
clearing (university entrance) **139**.30
clenbuterol hydrochloride **118**.35
climate change
    benefits **151**.6
    and biodiversity **146**.19, 21
    and British tourism **156**.28
    Climate Change Bill **151**.17
    Climate Change Programme **146**.8
    and consumerism **134**.31
    controversies **151**.3-6
    denial of **151**.12-13, 14-15
    effects of **151**.1, 6, 8, 9, 10
    and food production **140**.17, 37
    and forests **146**.30
    and global water supplies **76**.1, 3, 5, 8
    and globalisation **157**.10
    hypocrisy about **151**.12-13
    and inequality **151**.11, 19
    and meat production **140**.17
    natural **151**.3

Volume numbers appear first (in bold) followed by page numbers; a change in volume number is preceded by a semi-colon.

Vol. 76 The Water Crisis
Vol. 78 Threatened Species
Vol. 81 Alternative Therapies
Vol. 88 Food and Nutrition
Vol. 89 Refugees
Vol. 97 Energy Matters
Vol. 99 Exploited Children
Vol. 100 Stress and Anxiety
Vol. 107 Work Issues
Vol. 116 Grief and Loss
Vol. 118 Focus on Sport
Vol. 119 Transport Trends
Vol. 121 The Censorship Debate
Vol. 124 Parenting Issues
Vol. 125 Understanding Depression
Vol. 127 Eating Disorders
Vol. 128 The Cannabis Issue
Vol. 129 Gambling Trends
Vol. 130 Homelessness
Vol. 133 Teen Pregnancy and Lone Parents
Vol. 134 Customers and Consumerism
Vol. 135 Coping with Disability
Vol. 136 Self-Harm

Vol. 138 A Genetically Modified Future?
Vol. 139 The Education Problem
Vol. 140 Vegetarian and Vegan Diets
Vol. 141 Mental Health
Vol. 142 Media Issues
Vol. 143 Problem Drinking
Vol. 144 The Cloning Debate
Vol. 145 Smoking Trends
Vol. 146 Sustainability and Environment
Vol. 147 The Terrorism Problem
Vol. 148 Religious Beliefs
Vol. 149 A Classless Society?
Vol. 150 Migration and Population
Vol. 151 Climate Change
Vol. 152 Euthanasia and the Right to Die
Vol. 153 Sexual Orientation and Society
Vol. 154 The Gender Gap
Vol. 155 Domestic Abuse
Vol. 156 Travel and Tourism
Vol. 157 The Problem of Globalisation
Vol. 158 The Internet Revolution
Vol. 159 An Ageing Population
Vol. 160 Poverty and Exclusion

Vol. 161 Waste Issues
Vol. 162 Staying Fit
Vol. 163 Drugs in the UK
Vol. 164 The AIDS Crisis
Vol. 165 Bullying Issues
Vol. 166 Marriage and Cohabitation
Vol. 167 Our Human Rights
Vol. 168 Privacy and Surveillance
Vol. 169 The Animal Rights Debate
Vol. 170 Body Image and Self-Esteem
Vol. 171 Abortion – Rights and Ethics
Vol. 172 Racial and Ethnic Discrimination
Vol. 173 Sexual Health
Vol. 174 Selling Sex
Vol. 175 Citizenship and Participation
Vol. 176 Health Issues for Young People
Vol. 177 Crime in the UK
Vol. 178 Reproductive Ethics
Vol. 179 Tackling Child Abuse
Vol. 180 Money and Finances
Vol. 181 The Housing Issue

and nuclear power 97.19-20, 21, 22
political action 151.16-17, 27
and population control 151.31-2
public action 151.38-9
public awareness of factors contributing to 97.34
and renewable energy sources
bioenergy 97.18
case for 97.1-2
and wind energy 97.15
and species extinction 78.10, 11
and tourism 156.1, 25
tourist attitudes to 156.28-30
and transport emissions 119.14, 30
and water management 76.34
see also energy efficiency; global warming; greenhouse gas emissions
climate models 151.5
cloning
animals 144.30-39
definition 144.1, 4, 5, 18
ethical issues 144.2-3, 5-6, 7-8
and factory farming 144.35
and food production 144.36-9
how it works 144.1, 4, 14
human 144.1-14
natural 144.1
regulations 144.3
risks 144.2, 3, 6, 8
clothes
as economic indicator 180.5
recycling 161.28
CO₂ *see* carbon dioxide
co-parenting
after divorce 124.32
same-sex couples 178.9
coaches, sports
female 118.20
and pressure to use drugs 118.29
coal
and carbon allowances 151.37
as an energy source 97.4
coastal areas, effect of climate change 151.10
cocaine 163.4
street sales 163.12
use prevalence 163.7, 25
worldwide production 163.25
coffee growers and fairtrade 157.32, 33
cognitive ability and gender 154.24
Cognitive Behavioural Therapy (CBT) 141.35
and bipolar disorder 141.14-15
for bulimia nervosa (CBT-BN) 127.14
and giving up cannabis use 128.10
and self-harm 136.11
and Seasonal Affective Disorder 125.38
cohabitation 166.1, 12, 14-15
and expectation of marriage 166.2, 7
and stability for children 124.22
legal rights 166.12, 14-15
collagen, stem cell therapy 144.21-2
colour as grounds for discrimination 115.7
coming out 153.3, 8

commercial sexual exploitation of children 156.38-9
commercialisation
effect on children 134.11-12
in sport 118.9
commodification of children 178.12
'common law' marriages 166.12
communication
importance in bereavement 116.24-5
importance in depression 125.3, 39
young people 125.8
and eating disorders 127.30
trends 158.4-6
communications data 168.8, 13-14, 32-3
government database 168.13-14
privacy 168.2
community arts 141.38
community cohesion 131.2
community disclosure of sex offenders 179.20-21
community involvement, young people 131.32
Community Self Build 181.30-31
community sentences 177.17, 24, 25-6, 27-9
community orders 177.24, 25-6
community punishment orders 177.17
community rehabilitation orders 177.17
and knife crime 177.38
compensation for faulty goods 134.2, 17
compensation orders 177.17, 25
competition
and consumer choice 134.1
telecommunications industry 158.6
competition scams 134.26
competitive sport in schools 118.4
complaints
about goods 134.2, 17
complementary medicine (CM)
and consumer choice 81.37
and consumer ignorance 81.35
defining 81.1, 4
and depression 125.39
manic depression 125.20
and diagnosis 81.34
disciplines within 81.1-3
effectiveness of 81.22-4, 26, 27, 31
expenditure on 81.23, 37, 39
and GPs 81.21
impact on wildlife 78.23
and misdiagnosis 81.23
and multiple sclerosis 81.30-1
and the placebo effect 81.26, 28, 34
regulation of 81.23
safety of 81.27, 31
and scientists 81.28-9
and self-care 81.36-7
complex carbohydrates 88.2
composting waste 161.19, 28-9, 30
compulsions (obsessional rituals) 141.17
compulsive eating 127.20-21
compulsive exercise 162.39
compulsive gambling 129.2, 27-39
causes 129.29
definition 129.11

drug treatment **129**.39
    help for **129**.5, 29, 36, 37, 39
    online gambling **129**.21-2
    signs **129**.28, 29, 35-6, 38
    support groups **129**.37
    under 16s **129**.13, 25, 32-3
    women **129**.34
compulsive shopping **134**.13, 14
compulsory admission for eating disorders **127**.29
compulsory turnout to vote **131**.20-21
computer games
    violence, influence on children **121**.32-3, 35
computers
    and euthanasia decision-making **152**.38-9
    home computer ownership **134**.5
    recycling **161**.29
    spyware as tool of domestic abuse **155**.15-16
    see also Internet
conception **133**.8; **178**.2-3
    rate, young people **133**.2; **173**.3
conciliation (mediation) **166**.26, 35, 38-9
condoms **173**.2, 24; **176**.27
    and HIV **164**.3
    and the prevention of STIs **173**.24
    safe use **173**.5, 26
    usage **164**.26; **173**.22
confidence **170**.1, 8-9
    see also self-esteem
confidentiality and eating disorders **127**.28
congenital adrenal hyperplasia **154**.1
congestion, traffic **119**.11
    congestion charging **119**.12, 34-5, 38
    rail **119**.35
    and road building **119**.12
conservation
    animal species **78**.11
    English environment **146**.32-3
    and the exotic pet trade **78**.21-2
    plant species **78**.17
    tree species **78**.12
    zoo conservation **78**.24-5
    see also endangered species; extinction

conspicuous compassion **116**.17-18
constitutional change, impact on national identity **131**.5, 6
construction industry
    and energy efficiency **97**.36
    sustainability **146**.11
    waste recycling **161**.23
consultancies, tourism **156**.9
consumer adultery **161**.8-9
consumer assurance **134**.33-4
consumer choice **134**.1
consumer credit debt **134**.4, 23
consumer durables **134**.3-4, 5
consumer organisations **134**.21
consumer rights **134**.1-2, 17-21
    faulty goods **134**.2, 17
    and guarantees **134**.18-19
    private sales and auctions **134**.20
    and safety **134**.2
    secondhand goods **134**.20
consumer spending **134**.3-4
    see also shopping
consumerism
    and body image **170**.30-31
    green consumerism **146**.38-9
    and mental health problems **134**.5
consumers **134**.1
    and animal welfare **140**.31, 33
    and child labour **99**.12
    ethical behaviour **134**.33-5
    and genetic modification **138**.9
    older people **159**.19
    rights *see* consumer rights
    satisfaction **134**.6
    spending *see* consumer spending
consumption
    sustainable **146**.7
    UK **150**.32
contact with children after divorce **166**.26, 37-8
contained (indoor) GMOs **138**.12
contamination
    groundwater **146**.36
    land **146**.22

Volume numbers appear first (in bold) followed by page numbers; a change in volume number is preceded by a semi-colon.

Vol. 76 The Water Crisis
Vol. 78 Threatened Species
Vol. 81 Alternative Therapies
Vol. 88 Food and Nutrition
Vol. 89 Refugees
Vol. 97 Energy Matters
Vol. 99 Exploited Children
Vol. 100 Stress and Anxiety
Vol. 107 Work Issues
Vol. 116 Grief and Loss
Vol. 118 Focus on Sport
Vol. 119 Transport Trends
Vol. 121 The Censorship Debate
Vol. 124 Parenting Issues
Vol. 125 Understanding Depression
Vol. 127 Eating Disorders
Vol. 128 The Cannabis Issue
Vol. 129 Gambling Trends
Vol. 130 Homelessness
Vol. 133 Teen Pregnancy and Lone Parents
Vol. 134 Customers and Consumerism
Vol. 135 Coping with Disability
Vol. 136 Self-Harm

Vol. 138 A Genetically Modified Future?
Vol. 139 The Education Problem
Vol. 140 Vegetarian and Vegan Diets
Vol. 141 Mental Health
Vol. 142 Media Issues
Vol. 143 Problem Drinking
Vol. 144 The Cloning Debate
Vol. 145 Smoking Trends
Vol. 146 Sustainability and Environment
Vol. 147 The Terrorism Problem
Vol. 148 Religious Beliefs
Vol. 149 A Classless Society?
Vol. 150 Migration and Population
Vol. 151 Climate Change
Vol. 152 Euthanasia and the Right to Die
Vol. 153 Sexual Orientation and Society
Vol. 154 The Gender Gap
Vol. 155 Domestic Abuse
Vol. 156 Travel and Tourism
Vol. 157 The Problem of Globalisation
Vol. 158 The Internet Revolution
Vol. 159 An Ageing Population
Vol. 160 Poverty and Exclusion

Vol. 161 Waste Issues
Vol. 162 Staying Fit
Vol. 163 Drugs in the UK
Vol. 164 The AIDS Crisis
Vol. 165 Bullying Issues
Vol. 166 Marriage and Cohabitation
Vol. 167 Our Human Rights
Vol. 168 Privacy and Surveillance
Vol. 169 The Animal Rights Debate
Vol. 170 Body Image and Self-Esteem
Vol. 171 Abortion – Rights and Ethics
Vol. 172 Racial and Ethnic Discrimination
Vol. 173 Sexual Health
Vol. 174 Selling Sex
Vol. 175 Citizenship and Participation
Vol. 176 Health Issues for Young People
Vol. 177 Crime in the UK
Vol. 178 Reproductive Ethics
Vol. 179 Tackling Child Abuse
Vol. 180 Money and Finances
Vol. 181 The Housing Issue

see also pollution
content sharing sites **142**.35
contraception **173**.1, 3, 5, 25; **176**.27
    failure **173**.5
    and young people **133**.1, 2, 17; **173**.9
    see also condoms; family planning; pill, contraceptive
contract sales **107**.22
control orders **147**.3
copycat behaviour, self-harm **136**.10
copyright
    and downloading **158**.35, 36
    and Freedom of Information Act **142**.19
coral trade **78**.21
coroner **116**.32
corporal punishment **167**.36-9; **179**.30-38
    arguments against **179**.34-7
    arguments for not criminalizing **179**.33
    and children's rights **167**.36-8; **179**.30, 31-2
    definition **179**.30, 34
    and discipline **179**.37
    effects **179**.34
    government position **179**.33
    and the law **179**.30
    public opposition to **179**.32
    and religious views **179**.36
cosmetic surgery **170**.32-6
    reasons for **170**.35
    statistics **170**.34-5, 36
    and stem cell therapy **144**.24-5
    teenagers **170**.32-3, 36
cosmic rays and climate change **151**.6
cost of living **180**.6
costs
    academies **139**.15
    of ageing **159**.19-30
    of alcohol, effect on consumption **143**.17, 31
    of alcohol misuse **143**.36
    of the asylum system **89**.11, 30
    of cannabis **128**.2, 6
    of child poverty **160**.11
    of civil partnerships **153**.28
    of cleaner vehicles **119**.20-24
    of dementia **159**.35
    of disability **135**.5, 17, 18
    of domestic violence **155**.25
    of education **139**.1, 35; **160**.16-17, 19
    of fly-tipping **161**.16
    of free range food production **169**.11-12
    of fuel **160**.22-3
    of global warming **151**.8
    of home buying **181**.24
    of home care for the elderly **159**.26
    of identity cards **131**.13; **168**.17, 18-19
    of identity theft **168**.39
    of mental health problems **125**.16
    of motoring **119**.14
    of obesity **127**.33-4, 37
    of psychological therapy **125**.7
    of raising a child **124**.3
        as reason for smaller families **124**.18
    of smoking **145**.3, 17, 38

of social exclusion **149**.39
    university degrees **139**.35
    of vegan diet **140**.25
    of wasted food **161**.10-11
    of workplace bullying **165**.39
    of zero emission fuels **151**.28-9
cotinine **145**.26
cotton
    fairtrade **157**.28, 34
    genetically modified **138**.35
council tax
    benefit **135**.5
    and civil partnerships **153**.28
    lone parents **133**.35, 38
    and young people **181**.26
council tenants
    and right to move **181**.35-6
    rights **181**.16
    see also social housing
councils see local authorities
counselling **141**.35
    after abortion **171**.5
    for alcohol abuse **143**.25, 38
    for depression **125**.30-31
    eating disorders **127**.21, 29
    and help with stress **100**.32, 34
    for post-natal depression **125**.18
    and testing for HIV **96**.1
counter-terrorism **147**.2, 26-39
    and online activities **147**.9
    targeting terrorist funds **147**.3, 28-9
    UK strategy **147**.28-9
country of birth see birth country
countryside
    affordable housing **181**.3
    and the Hunting Act **169**.31-2
    and the production and use of energy **97**.24-5
coursework and Internet plagiarism **158**.19-20
courts of law
    divorce process **166**.36
    and torture evidence **167**.27
cows see cattle
crabs (pubic lice) **173**.17-18
crack cocaine **163**.4
    see also cocaine
cranial osteopathy **81**.2
creationism **148**.37
    teaching 36
creativity
    and help for self-harm **136**.3
    and mental health **141**.38
credit **180**.26-7
    consumer credit levels **134**.4, 23, 24
    credit purchases **180**.27
    and homeless young people **130**.25-6
    types of **134**.22; **180**.26-7
    unrequested **180**.15
    using wisely **134**.22
    see also debt
credit cards **134**.22, 24; **180**.14, 26
    and consumer rights **134**.18

international usage, women 180.19
  limits, unrequested increases 180.15
  store cards 180.14, 26
credit crunch 180.2-3, 4
  see also recession
cremation 116.37-8
crime 177.1-39
  and alcohol 176.15
  controlling movement of criminals in EU 150.7
  costs of 149.39
  cybercrime 158.35
  and domestic violence 155.2
  and drugs 163.2-3, 23
  and educational underachievement 149.39
  fear of 159.3; 177.2, 6, 20-21
  filesharing 158.36
  and forced marriages 155.17
  HIV transmission as crime 164.12-14
  identity theft 158.3
  levels of crime 177.20
  and licensing hours change 143.23
  and migrants 150.12, 13, 14
  and mobile phones 158.12-13
  phishing 158.36
  public worry about 177.2, 6, 20-21
  racially motivated 115.9-10
  religiously motivated 115.27; 148.29
  and surveillance 168.27
  victims of *see* victims of crime
  wildlife 78.19, 38-9
  youth crime, costs of 149.39
  see also fraud; victims of crime; violent crime; young offenders
crime prevention and CCTV 168.23-4
criminal justice system
  and domestic violence 155.35-8
  and gender equality 154.4
  youth courts 177.16-18
criminal responsibility, age of 177.19
criminality and mental health problems 125.16
crisis services, manic depression 125.20
crop biotechnology *see* genetically modified (GM) crops
crop rotation 88.14

cross-contamination, genetic 138.4
cross-cultural communication 142.34
cross-pollination, GM and non-GM crops 138.6-7, 12-13
cruises 156.1-2
cryogenic ID tags and IVF 178.22-3
cryopreservation *see* freezing
crystal meth (methamphetamine) 163.16-17, 32
CSA problems, single parent families 124.35
cultural capital 149.2
cultural Christianity 148.23-5
cultural differences and mixed-faith relationships 115.39
cultural traditions, British 131.1
culture
  and biological environment 146.19
  and body image 170.20
  and corporal punishment 179.36
  and domestic violence 155.4
  and gender discrimination 154.13-14
  and health inequalities 149.14
  and the media 142.34
  and religion 148.23-5
  effect of tourism 156.22
curfew orders 177.17, 25
current accounts 180.25
customer service satisfaction 134.6
customs, drugs seizures 163.37
cuts, first aid 136.22-3
cutting (self-harm), safety measures 136.22
cyanovirin-N 138.22
cyber safety 165.26-7, 30-31
cyberbullying 165.2, 9, 23-31
  anti-bullying strategies 165.25-6
  definitions 165.23, 25
  extent of 165.28, 29
  and the law 165.25
  preventing 165.25-6
  responding to 165.26
  at work 165.37-9
cybercrime 158.35
cyberterrorism 147.8-9
cybrids (animal-human hybrids) 144.9, 10-12
cycling 119.25, 29

Volume numbers appear first (in bold) followed by page numbers; a change in volume number is preceded by a semi-colon.

Vol. 76 The Water Crisis
Vol. 78 Threatened Species
Vol. 81 Alternative Therapies
Vol. 88 Food and Nutrition
Vol. 89 Refugees
Vol. 97 Energy Matters
Vol. 99 Exploited Children
Vol. 100 Stress and Anxiety
Vol. 107 Work Issues
Vol. 116 Grief and Loss
Vol. 118 Focus on Sport
Vol. 119 Transport Trends
Vol. 121 The Censorship Debate
Vol. 124 Parenting Issues
Vol. 125 Understanding Depression
Vol. 127 Eating Disorders
Vol. 128 The Cannabis Issue
Vol. 129 Gambling Trends
Vol. 130 Homelessness
Vol. 133 Teen Pregnancy and Lone Parents
Vol. 134 Customers and Consumerism
Vol. 135 Coping with Disability
Vol. 136 Self-Harm

Vol. 138 A Genetically Modified Future?
Vol. 139 The Education Problem
Vol. 140 Vegetarian and Vegan Diets
Vol. 141 Mental Health
Vol. 142 Media Issues
Vol. 143 Problem Drinking
Vol. 144 The Cloning Debate
Vol. 145 Smoking Trends
Vol. 146 Sustainability and Environment
Vol. 147 The Terrorism Problem
Vol. 148 Religious Beliefs
Vol. 149 A Classless Society?
Vol. 150 Migration and Population
Vol. 151 Climate Change
Vol. 152 Euthanasia and the Right to Die
Vol. 153 Sexual Orientation and Society
Vol. 154 The Gender Gap
Vol. 155 Domestic Abuse
Vol. 156 Travel and Tourism
Vol. 157 The Problem of Globalisation
Vol. 158 The Internet Revolution
Vol. 159 An Ageing Population
Vol. 160 Poverty and Exclusion

Vol. 161 Waste Issues
Vol. 162 Staying Fit
Vol. 163 Drugs in the UK
Vol. 164 The AIDS Crisis
Vol. 165 Bullying Issues
Vol. 166 Marriage and Cohabitation
Vol. 167 Our Human Rights
Vol. 168 Privacy and Surveillance
Vol. 169 The Animal Rights Debate
Vol. 170 Body Image and Self-Esteem
Vol. 171 Abortion – Rights and Ethics
Vol. 172 Racial and Ethnic Discrimination
Vol. 173 Sexual Health
Vol. 174 Selling Sex
Vol. 175 Citizenship and Participation
Vol. 176 Health Issues for Young People
Vol. 177 Crime in the UK
Vol. 178 Reproductive Ethics
Vol. 179 Tackling Child Abuse
Vol. 180 Money and Finances
Vol. 181 The Housing Issue

children 119.28; 124.14
health benefits 119.39
helmets 119.28
to school 119.30
cystic fibrosis research, animal experimentation 144.34

D

D notice 121.37
D&E (surgical dilation and evacuation) 171.3
daily benchmarks for alcohol consumption 143.8, 25, 26-7, 34
awareness of 143.11, 34
dairy foods 88.6, 15
dairy-free diet 140.22-3, 26
dark tourism 156.35-6
data protection
personal protection measures 168.31-2, 37
and self-regulation 168.2
Data Protection Act 168.10-11, 31, 37
day centres for homeless people 130.31
daylight, effect on mental health 141.35
death sites as tourist venues 156.35-6
death tourism 152.16
deaths
after abortion 171.6, 12
alcohol-related 143.3, 6, 37
cancer 81.23, 32
of children
cyclists 119.28
pedestrians 119.5, 30
children's questions about death 116.26-7
children's understanding of death 116.22
and drug misuse 163.11-12
formal procedures 116.29-32
in hospital 116.31
older people, winter 159.4
registering 116.31
in road accidents 119.4, 5, 30
from smoking 145.1, 4, 12, 22, 24
unexpected 116.31
from water-related diseases 76.2, 9, 13, 14, 20, 35
debit cards 134.24; 180.13, 26
debt 134.23-5; 160.32-3; 180.9-12
advice 134.23, 25; 180.27
affecting more affluent people 180.10
buying on credit 134.22
debt bondage 167.22
developing world 157.5, 9-10; 160.33
and homeless young people 130.24-6
icreasing incidence of debt 180.11
need for education about debt 180.38
and poverty 160.12
and social class 149.20
statistics 134.4, 23, 24; 180.9, 10, 11, 12
students 134.24
and young people 134.24
debt crisis 157.5; 180.10-12
decision-making
in euthanasia cases 152.38-9
young people 131.28

feelings of exclusion 131.26
decontamination of land, by plants 138.14
decree absolute 166.22, 26
decree nisi 166.22, 26
decriminalization of cannabis 128.7, 12
defensive verbalization 170.13
deferred sentences 177.18
deforestation 78.11, 18; 146.30-31
and water shortages 76.21, 36
degrees, university
costs 139.34, 35
courses 139.2, 29, 30, 38-9
and earnings 139.35, 36, 37
and ethnicity 139.8
and gender 139.10
results rising 139.33
delinquency, effect of divorce 124.34
dementia 141.6-8; 159.4, 35-9
and depression 125.5
fear of 159.39
statistics 125.16
see also Alzheimer's disease
democracy
and extremism 131.23-4
proposal for reform 131.25
see also elections
dental dams 96.2
dependency 141.9-10
depersonalisation 141.11
depressant drugs (downers) 163.2, 5-6
alcohol 143.4
see also cannabis; heroin; opiates; solvents
depression 125.1-23
and alcohol 125.2, 3, 36-7; 143.4
anti-depressant drugs see anti-depressant drugs
and body image 170.19
and cannabis use 128.14
causes of 125.2, 6, 19, 23
in children and young people 125.8, 9, 27-8; 176.30, 32
and complementary therapies 81.30, 31; 125.20, 39
endogenous 125.4
and exam stress 100.7
and exercise 125.3, 20, 39; 141.39; 162.37, 38
genetic factors in 125.2
and grief 116.5, 19
and incapacity benefit 100.23
manic depression see bipolar affective disorder
and men 125.13-15
in older people 125.22-3
and personality 125.2
and physical illness 125.2, 5-6
post-natal 125.4, 17-18
prevalence of 141.1, 2
reactive 125.4
seeking help 125.2-3
statistics on 136.33
and stress 100.1, 24
and suicide 125.10
symptoms of 125.1, 13
in the elderly 125.22-3
manic depression 125.19

post-natal depression **125**.17
seasonal affective disorder **125**.18
treatment of **125**.24-39
children and young people **125**.8, 27-8
diet **125**.3, 39
drugs **125**.7, 19, 22, 24-5, 32, 35
ECT (electroconvulsive therapy) **125**.25-6, 34, 35
elderly people **125**.23
manic depression **125**.19-20
post-natal depression **125**.17-18
psychotherapies **125**.29-31
Seasonal Affective Disorder **125**.18
self-help **125**.3, 39
talking therapies **125**.29-31
types of **125**.4
and underage drinking **125**.9
unipolar (endogenous) **125**.4, 10
young people **125**.8; **176**.30, 32
and university **176**.6
deprived areas as tourist sights **156**.33-5
derealisation **141**.11
desertification
causing migration **146**.16
and water shortages **76**.21, 36
designer babies **178**.31-2
designer holidays **156**.2
detention centres **89**.12, 13
detention and training orders **177**.17-18
detoxification **143**.38
developing countries
abortions **171**.11-12
ageing populations **159**.5
aid to *see* aid
and AIDS/HIV **96**.17-18, 36-7; **164**.10
alcohol consumption **143**.6
child labour in **99**.1, 2
and climate change action **151**.19
damaging effects of recycling **161**.35
debt and poverty **157**.9-10
and disability **135**.25, 26-7
effect of EU GM controls **138**.29-30
and free trade **157**.20, 25, 26-7

and gap years **156**.15-19
and globalisation **157**.25
and GM crops **138**.9, 10, 23, 34-5
money deposits in UK **146**.6
pensions **159**.24
receiving unwanted waste **161**.37
and the right to water **76**.24-5, 32
and smoking **145**.22-4
and tourism
problems **156**.22
slum tours **156**.33-5
sustainable tourism **156**.22-3
tourism dependency **156**.21
water collection **76**.13, 19-20
water pollution **76**.4, 10
water and sanitation services **76**.7, 8, 12, 17, 21
water shortages **76**.16, 19, 21
and agriculture **76**.3, 4
and aid programmes **76**.5
statistics **76**.2, 6, 7
and World Trade Organization **157**.22, 24
development
effect on environment **146**.24
and migration **150**.2
development aid, contributing to climate change **151**.27
devolution, effect on national identity **131**.5, 6
diabetes
and complementary therapies **81**.21
and obesity **127**.34
diarrhoea
and access to safe water and sanitation **76**.17
deaths from **76**.14, 30
and hygiene promotion **76**.6, 12
links to contaminated water **76**.5, 12
diet
and Buddhism **148**.11
and cancer treatments **81**.32-3
and Christianity **148**.2, 10
and depression **125**.3, 39
dietary trends **125**.11-12
healthy *see* healthy eating
and Hinduism **148**.3, 11

Volume numbers appear first (in bold) followed by page numbers; a change in volume number is preceded by a semi-colon.

Vol. 76 The Water Crisis
Vol. 78 Threatened Species
Vol. 81 Alternative Therapies
Vol. 88 Food and Nutrition
Vol. 89 Refugees
Vol. 97 Energy Matters
Vol. 99 Exploited Children
Vol. 100 Stress and Anxiety
Vol. 107 Work Issues
Vol. 116 Grief and Loss
Vol. 118 Focus on Sport
Vol. 119 Transport Trends
Vol. 121 The Censorship Debate
Vol. 124 Parenting Issues
Vol. 125 Understanding Depression
Vol. 127 Eating Disorders
Vol. 128 The Cannabis Issue
Vol. 129 Gambling Trends
Vol. 130 Homelessness
Vol. 133 Teen Pregnancy and Lone Parents
Vol. 134 Customers and Consumerism
Vol. 135 Coping with Disability
Vol. 136 Self-Harm

Vol. 138 A Genetically Modified Future?
Vol. 139 The Education Problem
Vol. 140 Vegetarian and Vegan Diets
Vol. 141 Mental Health
Vol. 142 Media Issues
Vol. 143 Problem Drinking
Vol. 144 The Cloning Debate
Vol. 145 Smoking Trends
Vol. 146 Sustainability and Environment
Vol. 147 The Terrorism Problem
Vol. 148 Religious Beliefs
Vol. 149 A Classless Society?
Vol. 150 Migration and Population
Vol. 151 Climate Change
Vol. 152 Euthanasia and the Right to Die
Vol. 153 Sexual Orientation and Society
Vol. 154 The Gender Gap
Vol. 155 Domestic Abuse
Vol. 156 Travel and Tourism
Vol. 157 The Problem of Globalisation
Vol. 158 The Internet Revolution
Vol. 159 An Ageing Population
Vol. 160 Poverty and Exclusion

Vol. 161 Waste Issues
Vol. 162 Staying Fit
Vol. 163 Drugs in the UK
Vol. 164 The AIDS Crisis
Vol. 165 Bullying Issues
Vol. 166 Marriage and Cohabitation
Vol. 167 Our Human Rights
Vol. 168 Privacy and Surveillance
Vol. 169 The Animal Rights Debate
Vol. 170 Body Image and Self-Esteem
Vol. 171 Abortion – Rights and Ethics
Vol. 172 Racial and Ethnic Discrimination
Vol. 173 Sexual Health
Vol. 174 Selling Sex
Vol. 175 Citizenship and Participation
Vol. 176 Health Issues for Young People
Vol. 177 Crime in the UK
Vol. 178 Reproductive Ethics
Vol. 179 Tackling Child Abuse
Vol. 180 Money and Finances
Vol. 181 The Housing Issue

and Islam **148**.3-4, 11
and Judaism **148**.4, 10-11
and mental health **125**.11-12; **141**.30-31, 34
and religion **148**.10-11
and Seasonal Affective Disorder **125**.38
and Sikhism **148**.5
and stress **100**.19, 30, 31, 35
and weight loss **162**.2
worldwide changes **162**.6
young people **176**.8-9
see also eating disorders; food and nutrition; healthy
eating; veganism; vegetarianism
diet industry and body image **170**.31
dietary obsession (orthorexia nervosa) **127**.19
digital entertainment **158**.3, 5, 7, 21-2
digital radio **158**.5
digital television **158**.5
dignity *see* human dignity
direct debits **180**.14
direct discrimination **153**.37-8
direct mail scams **134**.26-8
direct racial discrimination **115**.7, 11
disability
and abortion **171**.22
benefits **135**.3, 4, 5-6
and bullying **165**.9, 14-17
costs of **135**.5, 17, 18
definition **135**.2
discrimination **135**.1, 3, 28-9
workplace **135**.15
and employment **107**.12; **135**.3, 4, 14, 15
and the media **135**.29, 32, 35
and poverty **135**.16, 17-18; **160**.10, 25
public attitudes to **135**.1, 30-31
UK statistics **135**.1, 2-3, 6
worldwide statistics **135**.25
disability rights, UN treaty **135**.26
disability symbol **135**.14
disabled children **107**.21
choice in education **135**.24-5
in developing countries **135**.26
resources for **135**.21
violence against **135**.27
disabled people
and assisted suicide **152**.20-21
bullying of **165**.9, 14-17
discrimination **135**.1, 3
and employment **107**.12; **135**.3, 4, 14, 15
and football **118**.22
and transport **135**.7-9
see also disability; learning disabilities
disabled person's railcard **135**.8
disablism **135**.28-9
see also discrimination, disabled people
disaster victims, older people **159**.6
discharges (criminal) **177**.17, 24-5
discipline
parental **124**.2
see also corporal punishment; smacking
discrimination
and child labour **99**.4

direct and indirect **115**.7, 11
disabled people **135**.1, 3, 15, 28-9
see also Disability Discrimination Act **135**.13, 22, 31, 38-9
against middle class university applications **149**.7
and obesity **162**.21
racial *see* racial discrimination
sexual orientation **153**.2-3
in employment **153**.37-8
by social class **149**.2
in the workplace **135**.15; **153**.37-8
see also prejudice; racism; religious discrimination;
sex discrimination
disease
Millennium Development Goals **160**.32
water-related **76**.2, 3, 5, 6, 9, 12, 19, 20, 35; **146**.14, 15
and children **76**.2, 3, 5, 9, 13
displaced persons **89**.1, 6, 8-9
disposable nappies, waste **161**.1, 5, 29
disruptive behaviour disorder, influence of media violence
121.35
dissociative disorders **141**.11-13
distraction techniques, self-harmers **136**.5, 16, 19, 21
diuretics **118**.35, 37
diversity
as business benefit **135**.14
and sport **118**.12
divorce **166**.3, 21-39
and children **124**.29-30, 32, 33-4; **166**.4-5, 29-31, 32, 34-8
and duration of marriage **166**.27, 28
emotional effects **166**.22-4
how to help **166**.24
legal process **166**.22
and male depression **125**.14
reasons for **166**.21-2
risk factors **166**.28
statistics **166**.3, 4, 6, 25, 27, 28
DIY abortions **171**.35-6
DIY burials **116**.38-9
DNA **138**.4, 12; **144**.17; **168**.7, 11-12
DNA database **177**.31-2
doctors
and abortion **171**.25-8
and bereavement support **116**.2
and complementary medicine**81**.4
and disability support **135**.4
and euthanasia **152**.7, 8, 24-6, 27-8
fears of rise in gambling **129**.31
and help for eating disorders **127**.28
and reporting a death **116**.31
see also GPs (general practitioners); physician-assisted
suicide (PAS)
doctrine of double effect **152**.1, 3, 5
Dolly the sheep **144**.1, 15, 30-31, 32, 34, 39
domestic abuse **124**.18; **155**.1-39
convictions **155**.36-7
definitions **155**.1, 27
help for perpetrators **155**.33-4
helplines **133**.37; **155**.28-9
and housing support **130**.30
impact on children **155**.1, 4, 5, 19-25
injuries sustained **155**.30

leaving home **155**.4-5, 6-7, 12-13, 27-8
legal protection **155**.28
male victims **155**.12-13
myths and stereotypes **155**.3-5
personal stories **155**.8-10, 22-4
prevalence of **154**.12; **155**.5,10
register of offenders **155**.39
reluctance to seek help **155**.3-4, 5, 6, 7, 30-31
same-sex relationships **155**.13-15
seeking help **155**.3-4, 7, 30-31
signs of abuse **155**.1-2
statistics **155**.24-5
support for victims **155**.6-7, 28-9
tackling abuse **155**.27-39
and young people **155**.21, 26
domestic appliances, household ownership **134**.3-4, 5
domestic violence and teenagers **179**.19
domestic workers
    children as **99**.1, 4, 7-10; **167**.32
    migrant workers **150**.15
    slavery **167**.22, 32
donor insemination **178**.9
donors, eggs and sperm
    contact with offspring **178**.25, 26-7
    donor anonymity **178**.11, 24
    numbers falling **178**.24
    and parental rights **153**.34
dopamine **141**.9
doping *see* drugs in sport
Down's syndrome
    and Alzheimer's disease **141**.7
    and learning disabilities **135**.33
downloading **158**.35-6
dress code
    Christianity **148**.2
    Hinduism **148**.3
    Islam **148**.4
    Judaism **148**.4
    Sikhism **148**.5
drink-driving **119**.8-9; **143**.23-4
    alcohol limit **143**.3, 4
driver behaviour **119**.7-9

driving
    and alcohol *see* drink-driving
    and cannabis use **128**.14
    and disabled people **135**.4, 7
    driving licences, EU **168**.9
    and mobile phones **158**.12
drug abuse **128**.11; **163**.1, 3, 7; **176**.6, 19
    and abortion **171**.9
    costs **163**.21
    deaths from **163**.11-12
    declining **163**.22
    and fertility **178**.4, 5
    frequency **163**.3
    and HIV **96**.14, 26; **164**.17, 25
    and homeless people **130**.11, 20
    parents' worries about **124**.17
    and sex **173**.15
    and smoking **176**.12
    statistics **163**.3, 7, 24, 32; **176**.18
    worldwide **163**.25
    young people **163**.3, 15-16, 18-19, 26-30; **176**.6, 18
drug addiction **163**.2
drug development
    and animal experiments *see* animal experiments
    use of stem cells **144**.18
drug misuse **163**.1
drug overdoses **163**.12
    first aid **136**.23
    statistics **136**.26
drug rehabilitation orders for offenders **177**.18, 26
drug testing **118**.25
    statistics **118**.33-4
    UK **118**.28, 30
    at work **128**.20; **168**.38
drug treatment and testing orders **177**.18
drug treatments
    for depression **125**.7, 22, 32, 35
        manic depression **125**.19
        see also anti-depressants
    for gambling **129**.39
drugs
    for abortion **171**.2, 35, 36

Volume numbers appear first (in bold) followed by page numbers; a change in volume number is preceded by a semi-colon.

Vol. 76 The Water Crisis
Vol. 78 Threatened Species
Vol. 81 Alternative Therapies
Vol. 88 Food and Nutrition
Vol. 89 Refugees
Vol. 97 Energy Matters
Vol. 99 Exploited Children
Vol. 100 Stress and Anxiety
Vol. 107 Work Issues
Vol. 116 Grief and Loss
Vol. 118 Focus on Sport
Vol. 119 Transport Trends
Vol. 121 The Censorship Debate
Vol. 124 Parenting Issues
Vol. 125 Understanding Depression
Vol. 127 Eating Disorders
Vol. 128 The Cannabis Issue
Vol. 129 Gambling Trends
Vol. 130 Homelessness
Vol. 133 Teen Pregnancy and Lone Parents
Vol. 134 Customers and Consumerism
Vol. 135 Coping with Disability
Vol. 136 Self-Harm

Vol. 138 A Genetically Modified Future?
Vol. 139 The Education Problem
Vol. 140 Vegetarian and Vegan Diets
Vol. 141 Mental Health
Vol. 142 Media Issues
Vol. 143 Problem Drinking
Vol. 144 The Cloning Debate
Vol. 145 Smoking Trends
Vol. 146 Sustainability and Environment
Vol. 147 The Terrorism Problem
Vol. 148 Religious Beliefs
Vol. 149 A Classless Society?
Vol. 150 Migration and Population
Vol. 151 Climate Change
Vol. 152 Euthanasia and the Right to Die
Vol. 153 Sexual Orientation and Society
Vol. 154 The Gender Gap
Vol. 155 Domestic Abuse
Vol. 156 Travel and Tourism
Vol. 157 The Problem of Globalisation
Vol. 158 The Internet Revolution
Vol. 159 An Ageing Population
Vol. 160 Poverty and Exclusion

Vol. 161 Waste Issues
Vol. 162 Staying Fit
Vol. 163 Drugs in the UK
Vol. 164 The AIDS Crisis
Vol. 165 Bullying Issues
Vol. 166 Marriage and Cohabitation
Vol. 167 Our Human Rights
Vol. 168 Privacy and Surveillance
Vol. 169 The Animal Rights Debate
Vol. 170 Body Image and Self-Esteem
Vol. 171 Abortion – Rights and Ethics
Vol. 172 Racial and Ethnic Discrimination
Vol. 173 Sexual Health
Vol. 174 Selling Sex
Vol. 175 Citizenship and Participation
Vol. 176 Health Issues for Young People
Vol. 177 Crime in the UK
Vol. 178 Reproductive Ethics
Vol. 179 Tackling Child Abuse
Vol. 180 Money and Finances
Vol. 181 The Housing Issue

and alcohol **143**.3, 10
classification **163**.2, 31, 33-4, 37
  cannabis **163**.32, 35-6
  criticism of **163**.32
and crime **163**.2-3, 23, 38
definitions **163**.1, 31
and dependency **141**.9
depression caused by **125**.5-6, 10
effects
  amphetamines **163**.4-5
  cannabis **163**.6, 9, 35-6
  cocaine **163**.4
  ecstasy **163**.5, 9-10
  ketamine **163**.19-20
  LSD **163**.6
  magic mushrooms **163**.6
  opiates **163**.5
  solvents **163**.6
and fertility **178**.4, 5
and the law **163**.1-2, 31-9; **176**.19
and politics **163**.31-2
risks **143**.21-2
smuggling **163**.37-8
support for families of drug users **163**.24
types **163**.2
for weight loss **162**.2-3, 6, 20
and young people **163**.3, 9, 15-16; 18-19; 26-30
see also drug abuse
drugs in sport **118**.23-39
anabolic steroids **118**.35, 36
androstenedione **118**.35
athletes' responsibilities **118**.32-3
beta-blockers **118**.37
caffeine **118**.35
cannabinoids **118**.38
clenbuterol **118**.35
consequences of abuse **118**.32, 24
diuretics **118**.35, 37
effects of drugs **118**.35-8
ephedrine **118**.35
erythropoetin **118**.35
history of **118**.23-5
hormones **118**.37
medication and banned substances **118**.32-3
nadrolone precursors **118**.35
nalbuphine **118**.35
narcotic analgesics **118**.38
peptide hormones and analogues **118**.37
pressure to take drugs **118**.28-9
stimulants **118**.36-7
see also drug testing
DVDs, recycling **161**.23

E

e-commerce, Europe **134**.15-16
e-learning **139**.28
e-mail
  bullying **165**.23-4, 38-9
  phishing **134**.27-8, 28-9

  security measures **134**.28
  surveillance of **168**.8
early medical abortion (EMA) **171**.26
earnings
  effect of education **139**.1
  gender gap *see* gender pay gap
  graduates **139**.35, 36, 37
    and social class **149**.2
  minimum wage **107**.31
  teachers **139**.12
  see also incomes; salaries; wages
eating disorders **127**.1-31; **176**.9, 30, 39
  and body image **170**.19
  and compulsive exercise **162**.39
  and going to university **176**.6
  see also anorexia nervosa; bulimia nervosa; obesity
eco-lodges **156**.24
ecological debt **146**.4-6; **150**.32
ecological footprints **146**.10, 17
ecological overshoot **146**.10
economic globalisation **157**.2
economic growth
  costs of **157**.13
  and globalisation **157**.36-7
  impact of educational underachievement **149**.39
  impact of immigration **150**.11, 17
  indicators of recovery **180**.5
economic migrants and homelessness **130**.19
economy
  recession **180**.1-5
  and refugees **89**.21, 22, 30-1
  and tobacco **145**.22-3
ecosystems
  biodiversity **146**.18,19
  and climate change **151**.9
  degradation of freshwater **76**.35
  and water consumption **76**.2, 16-17, 19
ecotourism **156**.20, 24
eco-towns **151**.32; **181**.36-9
eco-travel spending **134**.32
ecstasy (MDMA) **163**.5, 9-10
  deaths fron **163**.11
  and depression **125**.10
  risks **143**.22
  safety **163**.34
  street sales **163**.12-13
  use, Europe **163**.25
ECT (electro-convulsive therapy) **125**.25-6, 34, 35
education **139**.1-39
  on abortion **171**.36-9
  and alcohol **143**.20
  and black history **115**.16-17
  and black pupils **115**.19-21
  and the Budget **180**.24
  effects of cannabis use **128**.14
  and child labour **99**.3, 7, 15; **167**.31
  and child soldiers **99**.31
  costs **124**.3; **139**.1; **160**.16-17
  and disabled children **135**.24-5, 26; 36-9
  on drugs **163**.24
  and earnings **139**.1, 35, 36, 37

and ethnicity 139.8-9
faith-based schools 148.34, 35-6
and family income 149.25
financial 180.36-9
and gender 139.10-11; 154.12, 22-7
global gender inequality 154.12
higher education 139.29-39
  government funding 180.28, 33
about HIV 164.18, 23-4
home learning 139.27-8
and homeless people
  level of education 130.15
  needs 130.34-5
as a human right 167.23
on intelligent design 148.39
and learning disabilities 135.36-9
in mental health 141.37
Millennium Development Goals 160.30-31
and minority ethnic pupils 115.18
multi-faith schools 148.32-3
and parents' mental health problems 141.24
PE 118.3
personal, social and health education 133.16
and poverty 160.2, 17-22
and racial integration 115.29, 30, 37
and racism 115.19-20
and smoking 145.3
and social division 177.4
and social mobility 139.13; 149.22, 25, 30, 36-7
special educational needs (SEN) 135.36-9
statistics 139.1-2
teaching happiness 170.14-15
and teenage mothers 133.24
underachievement, costs of 149.39
and war-affected children 99.34
and young people with HIV/AIDS 96.26, 32, 33
see also educational achievement; schools; sex education;
  students; teachers; universities
educational achievement
black pupils 115.20
and ethnicity 139.8
and family income 149.25

gender differences 154.22, 23
effect of poverty 160.2, 18-19, 20, 21
and school pupil intake 149.31-3
and single-sex schooling 139.11-12
and social class 149.30, 31-3
see also exam results
egg donation 178.10-12
for embryonic stem cell research 178.34-5
numbers declining 178.24
risks 178.12
egg freezing 178.23
eggs
consumer choices 140.37-8
free-range 140.6, 29, 38-9
from GM hens, and cancer treatment 138.20-21
and health 140.30, 39
production methods 140.29, 38-9
sales 140.37-8
and vegetarian diets 140.6, 19, 26
ejaculation 178.3
disorders 178.5
elderly people
and dementia see dementia
and depression 125.22-3
elder abuse 159.4, 6, 16-18
and homelessness 130.17-18
and mental health problems 141.2
see also ageing population; grandparents; older people
elections 131.16-22
campaigns 131.18
European 131.15
General Elections 131.18
terminology 131.17
voter turnout 131.19-21
electoral register 131.16
electoral system 131.15-26
electric hybrid vehicles 119.22
electric vehicles 119.21-2
electro-convulsive therapy (ECT) 125.25-6, 34, 35
electronic equipment recycling 161.8-9, 23-4
electronic footprints 158.10-11
embarkation controls 150.7

Volume numbers appear first (in bold) followed by page numbers; a change in volume number is preceded by a semi-colon.

Vol. 76 The Water Crisis
Vol. 78 Threatened Species
Vol. 81 Alternative Therapies
Vol. 88 Food and Nutrition
Vol. 89 Refugees
Vol. 97 Energy Matters
Vol. 99 Exploited Children
Vol. 100 Stress and Anxiety
Vol. 107 Work Issues
Vol. 116 Grief and Loss
Vol. 118 Focus on Sport
Vol. 119 Transport Trends
Vol. 121 The Censorship Debate
Vol. 124 Parenting Issues
Vol. 125 Understanding Depression
Vol. 127 Eating Disorders
Vol. 128 The Cannabis Issue
Vol. 129 Gambling Trends
Vol. 130 Homelessness
Vol. 133 Teen Pregnancy and Lone Parents
Vol. 134 Customers and Consumerism
Vol. 135 Coping with Disability
Vol. 136 Self-Harm

Vol. 138 A Genetically Modified Future?
Vol. 139 The Education Problem
Vol. 140 Vegetarian and Vegan Diets
Vol. 141 Mental Health
Vol. 142 Media Issues
Vol. 143 Problem Drinking
Vol. 144 The Cloning Debate
Vol. 145 Smoking Trends
Vol. 146 Sustainability and Environment
Vol. 147 The Terrorism Problem
Vol. 148 Religious Beliefs
Vol. 149 A Classless Society?
Vol. 150 Migration and Population
Vol. 151 Climate Change
Vol. 152 Euthanasia and the Right to Die
Vol. 153 Sexual Orientation and Society
Vol. 154 The Gender Gap
Vol. 155 Domestic Abuse
Vol. 156 Travel and Tourism
Vol. 157 The Problem of Globalisation
Vol. 158 The Internet Revolution
Vol. 159 An Ageing Population
Vol. 160 Poverty and Exclusion

Vol. 161 Waste Issues
Vol. 162 Staying Fit
Vol. 163 Drugs in the UK
Vol. 164 The AIDS Crisis
Vol. 165 Bullying Issues
Vol. 166 Marriage and Cohabitation
Vol. 167 Our Human Rights
Vol. 168 Privacy and Surveillance
Vol. 169 The Animal Rights Debate
Vol. 170 Body Image and Self-Esteem
Vol. 171 Abortion – Rights and Ethics
Vol. 172 Racial and Ethnic Discrimination
Vol. 173 Sexual Health
Vol. 174 Selling Sex
Vol. 175 Citizenship and Participation
Vol. 176 Health Issues for Young People
Vol. 177 Crime in the UK
Vol. 178 Reproductive Ethics
Vol. 179 Tackling Child Abuse
Vol. 180 Money and Finances
Vol. 181 The Housing Issue

embryo cloning *see* human reproductive cloning
embryo donation **144**.7
    for research **178**.37
embryo freezing, effects on health **178**.22
embryo selection **178**.28-32
embryonic stem cell research **144**.2
    Catholic Church opposition **178**.35
    ethical issues **144**.6; **178**.33-5
    humanist view **144**.7-8, **178**.36-7
    see also therapeutic cloning
embryos
    hybrid **144**.9, 11, 14, 20; **178**.35
    moral status **178**.33-4
emergency contraception **173**.5, 25; **176**.27
emergency treatment
    self-harmers **136**.22-3
emigrants
    British **150**.24-5
    definition **150**.21
emissions
  calculations **151**.22
    reduction **151**.2, 13, 17, 36-7
    transport **119**.1, 15, 31
    aircraft **119**.16
    and climate change **119**.14, 24, 30
emotional abuse **155**.3; **179**.1
    signs of **179**.5
emotional blackmail by parents **124**.15
emotional changes, and stress **100**.33
emotional disorders, young people **125**.9
emotional distress as cause of eating disorders **127**.2
emotional health
    problems of consumerism **134**.5
    see also mental health
emotional impact
    of abortion **171**.5
    of divorce **166**.22-4
    of domestic violence **155**.30
    of poor body image **170**.19
emotional literacy classes **141**.37
emotional skills **170**.5
emotions, animals **140**.27-8; **169**.2-3
employees
    gambling at work **129**.22-4
    surveillance **168**.9.27, 38
employers
    basic skills requirements **139**.17
    equality policies **115**.13
    liability for racism **115**.12
    links with higher education **139**.38-9
    workforce monitoring by GPS **168**.27
    workplace monitoring **168**.38
    and workplace stress **100**.17-18, 20
employment
    and age discrimination **159**.8-13
    barriers to **160**.13
    census information **150**.36
    difficulty finding jobs **180**.34-5
    of disabled people **107**.12; **135**.3, 4, 14, 15
    as economic indicator **180**.5
    effect of free trade **157**.13, 23

    effects of recession **180**.3
    and gender **154**.29-35
    effect of globalisation **157**.36-7
    graduates **139**.33
    and homeless people **130**.15, 36-7
    inequalities **149**.28
    and lone parents **133**.28
    and mental illness **141**.22
    effect of migration **150**.9-10
    and obesity discrimination **162**.21
    from recycling **161**.2
    past retirement age **159**.10, 15
    and racism **115**.12, 13
    sexual orientation discrimination **153**.37-9
    students **139**.35; **180**.29
    tourism industry **156**.10
    working conditions, international companies **157**.11
    young people and the law **180**.20
        see also hours of work; jobs; part-time jobs; unemployment;
            women in the workforce; work-life balance; workplace
            bullying; workplace stress
employment of refugees **89**.22-3, 24, 26-7, 32
    illegal employment of refugees **89**.10-11, 30-1
endangered species **78**.1-3
    birds **78**.2, 8-9, 27, 29, 37
    and the killing of wildlife **78**.2, 4-5, 5-6
    mammals **78**.3, 27, 28, 32
    plants **78**.2-3, 7, 17, 21, 36
    and pollution **78**.6
    trade in **78**.16-17, 19-22, 38-9
    in the UK **78**.28-31
    see also conservation; extinction; wildlife
endocrine disorders and depression **125**.5
endogenous (unipolar) depression **125**.4, 10
endometriosis **178**.4
energy
    and the countryside **97**.24-5
    and exercise **141**.39
    household costs and poverty **160**.22-3
    and meat-eating **140**.21
    output of the energy industry **97**.3
    production and supply **97**.3-4
    public attitudes to energy and environment **97**.34-6
    saving through recycling **161**.22
    from waste **161**.20, 38, 39
energy consumption **97**.6
    construction industry **146**.11
    increasing **146**.39
energy dependence of UK **146**.5-6
energy efficiency **97**.27-33; **151**.29
    and global warming **97**.29
    in the home **97**.2, 27-30, 31, 32-3; **151**.39; **181**.39
    and renewable energy sources **97**.11
    and shopping **97**.31-2
    and sustainable housing **181**.39
    and transport **97**.24, 25, 31
    see also renewable energy
entertainment and the Internet **158**.3, 7, 21-2
environment
    and agriculture **146**.25
    and air travel **156**.21, 26

effects of genetic modification **138**.12-14, 24
effect of globalisation **157**.10
information requests **142**.19
and meat production **140**.13, 16-7
effect of migration **150**.26-7
protection of **88**.32, 34, 35
public attitudes to **97**.34
sustainable housing **181**.39
and tobacco **145**.23
impact of tourism **156**.20, 21, 22, 25
   air travel **156**.21, 26
   reducing **156**.24
and transnational companies **157**.10-11
and urban growth **146**.17
and water bills **76**.33, 34
and World Trade Organisation **157**.22-3
see also sustainable development; wildlife
environmental globalisation **157**.2
environmental migration **146**.16-17
environmental motoring, Ford **134**.30
environmental sustainability *see* sustainability
environmental taxes **157**.12-13
environmental tobacco smoke *see* passive smoking
environmentally cleaner vehicles **119**.20-23
ephedrine **118**.35
equal opportunity in sport **118**.12-13, 15-16, 18-19, 22
equal pay *see* gender pay gap
equality rights, disabled people **135**.13
equity in sport **118**.12
   gender equity **118**.18-19
erythropoetin (EPO) **118**.35, 37
escalation theory of drug use **128**.9-10, 11, 28
established church **148**.21-2
estimates and consumer rights **134**.18
ethical consumerism **134**.30-38
ethical food **134**.32, 34-7
ethical trade **134**.36; **157**.18
   see also fair trade
ethical travel **134**.30
ethics
   and animal experiments **169**.15-16
   of genetic modification **138**.23

of human cloning **144**.2-3, 5-6, 7-8
ethnic groups interaction **147**.19
ethnic minorities
   British identity **115**.38
   and community feelings **131**.2
   and country of birth **131**.8
   and education **115**.18; **139**.8-9
   and football **118**.13-16
   interest in the news **142**.32-3
   and mental illness **141**.23
   mixed race population in the UK **115**.24-5
   and national identity **131**.1, 8
   and racial discrimination perception **131**.2-3
   social mobility **149**.21-2
   and the UK census **115**.3
   as victims of crime **115**.10
   see also Asian people; black people; employment and racism; racism
ethnic origin
   and age of population, UK **150**.39
   census data **150**.36
   and education **139**.8-9
   gender and educational achievement **154**.23
   gender and pupil behaviour **154**.24
   as grounds for discrimination **115**.7
   homeless people **130**.10, 14
   and poverty **160**.2
   women in the workforce **154**.29
European Convention on Human Rights **167**.4
   and privacy **168**.3
   and sexuality **153**.30-31
European Court of Human Rights **153**.31
   and DNA records **168**.12
   and gay adoption **153**.31
   and parental rights **153**.34
   and privacy **168**.3
European Union
   accession countries, migration from **150**.6-7
   ban on advertising tobacco **145**.7
   and biotechnology **138**.28-9
   carbon credits **151**.35, 37
Technological Innovation **142**.1

Volume numbers appear first (in bold) followed by page numbers; a change in volume number is preceded by a semi-colon.

Vol. 76 The Water Crisis
Vol. 78 Threatened Species
Vol. 81 Alternative Therapies
Vol. 88 Food and Nutrition
Vol. 89 Refugees
Vol. 97 Energy Matters
Vol. 99 Exploited Children
Vol. 100 Stress and Anxiety
Vol. 107 Work Issues
Vol. 116 Grief and Loss
Vol. 118 Focus on Sport
Vol. 119 Transport Trends
Vol. 121 The Censorship Debate
Vol. 124 Parenting Issues
Vol. 125 Understanding Depression
Vol. 127 Eating Disorders
Vol. 128 The Cannabis Issue
Vol. 129 Gambling Trends
Vol. 130 Homelessness
Vol. 133 Teen Pregnancy and Lone Parents
Vol. 134 Customers and Consumerism
Vol. 135 Coping with Disability
Vol. 136 Self-Harm

Vol. 138 A Genetically Modified Future?
Vol. 139 The Education Problem
Vol. 140 Vegetarian and Vegan Diets
Vol. 141 Mental Health
Vol. 142 Media Issues
Vol. 143 Problem Drinking
Vol. 144 The Cloning Debate
Vol. 145 Smoking Trends
Vol. 146 Sustainability and Environment
Vol. 147 The Terrorism Problem
Vol. 148 Religious Beliefs
Vol. 149 A Classless Society?
Vol. 150 Migration and Population
Vol. 151 Climate Change
Vol. 152 Euthanasia and the Right to Die
Vol. 153 Sexual Orientation and Society
Vol. 154 The Gender Gap
Vol. 155 Domestic Abuse
Vol. 156 Travel and Tourism
Vol. 157 The Problem of Globalisation
Vol. 158 The Internet Revolution
Vol. 159 An Ageing Population
Vol. 160 Poverty and Exclusion

Vol. 161 Waste Issues
Vol. 162 Staying Fit
Vol. 163 Drugs in the UK
Vol. 164 The AIDS Crisis
Vol. 165 Bullying Issues
Vol. 166 Marriage and Cohabitation
Vol. 167 Our Human Rights
Vol. 168 Privacy and Surveillance
Vol. 169 The Animal Rights Debate
Vol. 170 Body Image and Self-Esteem
Vol. 171 Abortion – Rights and Ethics
Vol. 172 Racial and Ethnic Discrimination
Vol. 173 Sexual Health
Vol. 174 Selling Sex
Vol. 175 Citizenship and Participation
Vol. 176 Health Issues for Young People
Vol. 177 Crime in the UK
Vol. 178 Reproductive Ethics
Vol. 179 Tackling Child Abuse
Vol. 180 Money and Finances
Vol. 181 The Housing Issue

child abuse laws **179**.29
citizenship **131**.38
    and corporal punishment legislation **179**.31
elections **131**.15
entry-exit system **168**.9
GM ban, effect on developing countries **138**.29-30
human rights treaties **168**.3
and ID cards **131**.13
smoking **145**.21
students from EU countries **139**.30, 32
surveillance in **168**.9
trafficking laws **179**.29
views of young people **131**.39
and wildlife trade **146**.34
workplace gender gap **154**.17-18, 33
euthanasia **152**.1-39
    active **152**.5
    arguments against **152**.3-4, 5, 17-18
    arguments for **152**.3-4, 6, 10
    and treatment of babies **152**.4, 32, 33, 34
    definitions **152**.1, 2, 5, 19
    diminishing respect for life **152**.3-4
    involuntary **152**.1
    law on **152**.1, 16-18, 29-30
    medical profession's attitudes **152**.7, 8, 24-6, 27-8
    non-voluntary **152**.1, 3
    in other countries **152**.4, 18, 19, 31, 33
    and religious faith **152**.7, 12, 15
        Church of England **152**.34
        Roman Catholic Church **152**.3-4
    statistics **152**.17, 23, 24, 25
    see also advance directives; assisted suicide; physician
        assisted suicide (PAS)
eviction of tenants **181**.16
evidence obtained under torture **167**.27
evolution
    and animals **78**.1
    public opinions on **148**.37
exams **139**.4
    results
        A-levels **139**.18
        academies **139**.14, 15
        AS-levels **139**.18
        exceeding expectation **139**.22
        GCSEs **139**.2
    gender differences **154**.22, 23
        and single-sex schooling **139**.12; **154**.27
    standards **139**.19-20
    and stress **100**.3-7; **176**.5, 38-9
        causes of **100**.5
        dealing with **100**.5, 6
        getting help and advice with **100**.3
    see also A-levels; AS-levels; GCSEs
exchange rate, effect on tourism **156**.1, 7-8
exclusion clauses and consumer rights **134**.19-20
exclusions from school
    black pupils **115**.19-20; **139**.9
    and ethnicity **139**.8, 9
    gender differences **154**.24
exercise **88**.1, 2-3, 11, 12, 18; **162**.6; 29-34; **176**.6-7
    and the ageing process **159**.33; **162**.12

barriers to **162**.24, 29
benefits of **118**.3
    for women **118**.20
and body image **176**.7
children **119**.31; **162**.6, 26, 28, 29; **176**.3
    effect on weight **162**.28, 29
    lack of exercise **162**.13, 15, 25
compulsive **162**.39
and depression **125**.3, 20, 39; **162**.37, 38
and giving up smoking **145**.36
government strategy **162**.18
and health **162**.11-12, 29-31
influence of lads' magazines **170**.28
lack of *see* inactivity
and life expectancy **159**.33
and mental health **141**.34, 39; **162**.37, 38
motivation for **162**.30-31
and obesity **162**.28, 29, 36
older people **159**.39
recommended amounts **162**.30
statistics **162**.6
and stress
    benefits of **100**.19, 27, 30, 34, 36, 37
and weight loss **162**.20
when not to exercise **162**.31-2
in the workplace **162**.23, 24
and young people **176**.6-7
exhaust gases *see* emissions, transport
exploitation of workers
    migrant workers **150**.14, 15, 19, 20, 22
expression, freedom of *see* freedom of expression
extended schools **149**.30, 37-8
extended warranties **134**.19
external costs of motoring **119**.14
extra-curricular activities and social mobility **149**.30, 37-8
extremism
    monitoring extremist networks **147**.13-14
    tackling **147**.33-4; **148**.30-31
extremist parties **131**.23-4
    impact on democracy **131**.24

F

Facebook and privacy **168**.35
facial stem cell therapy **144**.21-2
factory farming and animal cloning **144**.35
fair trade **134**.34-7; **157**.18, 27, 31-4
    coffee **157**.32, 33
    cotton **157**.28, 34
    ineffectiveness **157**.34
Fairtrade Foundation **134**.34-5, 36-7; **157**.31
Fairtrade mark **134**.35, 37
faith-based bullying **165**.9
faith differences and relationships **115**.39
faith hate crime **115**.27
faith schools **148**.34, 35-6
    and sex education **173**.34-5
fallopian tube damage and infertility **178**.4
falls, older people **159**.4, 6
false memory syndrome **179**.26-9

families
    abuse of older people **159**.17
    adjusting to a new family **124**.31
    and drinking behaviour of young people **143**.5, 17
    changing family patterns **124**.20-39; **166**.15; **177**.2
    and debt problems **160**.12
    digital technology usage **158**.7-8
    and disability **135**.4
    of drug users, support for **163**.24
    equality issues **154**.3
    family conflict and street homelessness **130**.10
    and football **141**.33
    income, effect on educational attainment **149**.25
    of lesbians and gay people, support **153**.10
    low income, broadband access **158**.18
    and manic depressives **125**.20
    and mobile phones **158**.13
    and poverty **160**.13-14
    pressure on athletes to take drugs **118**.29
    problems **124**.18
    reaction to mixed-faith relationships **115**.39
    size
        influenced by costs of raising children **124**.18
    support during divorce **166**.29, 30, 31
    and working parents **124**.1, 21
    see also lone parents; parents; stepfamilies
family planning
    and teenagers **133**.2
    US overseas aid funding **171**.13-14
    see also birth control; contraception
family planning clinics, use by teenagers **173**.9
farming *see* agriculture; organic farming
fashion industry, employment conditions **157**.27-9
fasting
    Christianity **148**.10
    Islam **148**.11
fat **162**.8
    spot-reduction **162**.33
fat intake **88**.2, 5, 7, 8
    and food labelling **88**.21-2, 22-3
    and red meat **140**.12
fathers

    and childcare **124**.7-11
    impact on children's achievement **124**.7
    employment patterns **107**.24-5
    full-time fathers **124**.9-10
    and household tasks **124**.11
    new fathers and depression **125**.14
    paternity leave **107**.25
    rights and responsibilities **133**.39
    teenage fathers **133**.25-7
    unmarried, and parental responsibility **124**.4
    working fathers **107**.24-25
fatty acids
    and ADHD (attention-deficit hyperactivity disorder) **141**.19
    in diet **141**.30
fatwa **147**.15
faulty goods, consumer rights **134**.17
fear of crime **177**.2, 6, 20-21
fear of terrorism **147**.12
fear after traumatic bereavement **116**.11-12
fear of young people **177**.3, 22
feelings
    of animals **140**.27-8
    after bereavement **116**.1, 3-4, 5, 7-9, 10-11, 19, 21-2, 30
fees, university **139**.34
female condoms (femidom) **173**.24
fertility
    effect of abortion **171**.3
    effect of smoking **145**.32
    and environmental stress **146**.16-17
    problems **178**.2-5
    UK **151**.32
    worldwide **150**.32-3, 34
fertility tourism **178**.18, 20
fertility treatment, gay people **153**.33-4
festivals
    Buddhism **148**.2
    Christianity **148**.2
    Hinduism **148**.3
    Islam **148**.3
    Judaism **148**.4
    Sikhism **148**.5
fetus

Volume numbers appear first (in bold) followed by page numbers; a change in volume number is preceded by a semi-colon.

Vol. 76 The Water Crisis
Vol. 78 Threatened Species
Vol. 81 Alternative Therapies
Vol. 88 Food and Nutrition
Vol. 89 Refugees
Vol. 97 Energy Matters
Vol. 99 Exploited Children
Vol. 100 Stress and Anxiety
Vol. 107 Work Issues
Vol. 116 Grief and Loss
Vol. 118 Focus on Sport
Vol. 119 Transport Trends
Vol. 121 The Censorship Debate
Vol. 124 Parenting Issues
Vol. 125 Understanding Depression
Vol. 127 Eating Disorders
Vol. 128 The Cannabis Issue
Vol. 129 Gambling Trends
Vol. 130 Homelessness
Vol. 133 Teen Pregnancy and Lone Parents
Vol. 134 Customers and Consumerism
Vol. 135 Coping with Disability
Vol. 136 Self-Harm

Vol. 138 A Genetically Modified Future?
Vol. 139 The Education Problem
Vol. 140 Vegetarian and Vegan Diets
Vol. 141 Mental Health
Vol. 142 Media Issues
Vol. 143 Problem Drinking
Vol. 144 The Cloning Debate
Vol. 145 Smoking Trends
Vol. 146 Sustainability and Environment
Vol. 147 The Terrorism Problem
Vol. 148 Religious Beliefs
Vol. 149 A Classless Society?
Vol. 150 Migration and Population
Vol. 151 Climate Change
Vol. 152 Euthanasia and the Right to Die
Vol. 153 Sexual Orientation and Society
Vol. 154 The Gender Gap
Vol. 155 Domestic Abuse
Vol. 156 Travel and Tourism
Vol. 157 The Problem of Globalisation
Vol. 158 The Internet Revolution
Vol. 159 An Ageing Population
Vol. 160 Poverty and Exclusion

Vol. 161 Waste Issues
Vol. 162 Staying Fit
Vol. 163 Drugs in the UK
Vol. 164 The AIDS Crisis
Vol. 165 Bullying Issues
Vol. 166 Marriage and Cohabitation
Vol. 167 Our Human Rights
Vol. 168 Privacy and Surveillance
Vol. 169 The Animal Rights Debate
Vol. 170 Body Image and Self-Esteem
Vol. 171 Abortion – Rights and Ethics
Vol. 172 Racial and Ethnic Discrimination
Vol. 173 Sexual Health
Vol. 174 Selling Sex
Vol. 175 Citizenship and Participation
Vol. 176 Health Issues for Young People
Vol. 177 Crime in the UK
Vol. 178 Reproductive Ethics
Vol. 179 Tackling Child Abuse
Vol. 180 Money and Finances
Vol. 181 The Housing Issue

age of viability 171.23, 31, 33-4
    feeling pain 171.31, 34
    religious views on foetus 171.17-18
    testing for disability 171.22
fibre intake 88.2, 5, 6, 23
filesharing 158.36
films
    classification 121.22, 23-5, 29-30
    cuts 121.25
    online viewing 158.21-2
    and smoking 145.8-10
    violence, and playground bullying 121.28
financial abuse and older people 159.16
financial crisis, global 180.1-2
financial disruption to terrorism 147.3, 28
financial education 180.36-9
financial expectations, young people 180.20-21
financial freedom, older people 159.20
financial incentives
    for marriage 166.5
    for reducing waste 161.38
    for weight loss 162.22-3
financial planning for old age 159.21-2; 180.8
    see also pensions
financial problems as cause of street homelessness 130.11
financial responsibility for children 166.14-15, 34-5
financial support to adult children
    by grandmothers 124.38
    by parents 124.3
financial worries and non-traditional families 124.20
fine particles, air pollution 146.35
fines 177.17, 24
fingerprinting
    on arrest 177.36
    in schools 168.30
first aid 136.22-3
    for drug emergencies 136.23
first-time buyers
    parental support 181.1
    pessimism about owning homes 181.5
fishing
    and the protection of the oceans 78.14
    and sustainability 146.28-9
fitness
    effects on ageing 159.33, 34; 162.12
    equipment for older people 159.39
    government strategy 162.17-18
    inequalities 162.35
    and mental health 141.34, 39; 162.37, 38
    motivation 162.30-31
    myths 162.33-4
    see also exercise
fitness industry, lack of effect on obesity 162.35
fixed penalty notices 177.8, 25
Fleet Street and newspaper publishing 142.8-9
flexible working 107.2, 11-12, 14-19
    father-friendly employment 107.25
    and lone parents 133.38
    right to request 107.17-18, 21-2
flooding and climate change 151.10-11
fly-tipping 161.16

foetal stem cells 144.25
foetus see fetus
food
    and alcohol 143.7
    and animal cloning 144.36-9
    and energy efficiency 97.32, 33
    ethical 134.34-7
    food costs and animal welfare 169.11-12
    food security 146.12-13
    food value of alcohol 143.2
    GM food see genetically modified (GM) crops
    hunger see hunger
    and mental health 141.30-31, 34
    organic 134.31
    production and global water supplies 76.3, 4, 7, 18
    and religion 148.10-11
    supplies and GM crops 138.9, 10, 34-5
    UK dependence on imports 146.5
    and young people 176.8-9
    see also diet; eating disorders; fat intake; healthy eating;
        meat consumption; vegetarian food
food labelling 88.9, 21-5
    GM food 138.11, 39
food and nutrition 88.1-39
    additives 88.13-14, 34, 36, 38, 39
    advertising and promotion 88.10, 11, 19, 20, 35, 37
    food poisoning 88.14, 27-9
    food safety 88.26, 32, 34
    healthy diet 88.1-2, 5-7
    junk food 88.9-11
    locally grown produce 88.31, 33
    nutrition information panels 88.21, 22-3
    teenagers 176.8-9
    see also diet; healthy eating; nutrition; vegetarianism
food poisoning 88.14, 27-9
food production
    and intensive farming 140.36-7
    and meat consumption 140.13, 16-17
    and mental health 141.30
food waste 161.4, 10-11, 19
football
    and disabled people 118.22
    and girls' self-esteem 170.39
    and homophobia 118.17
    and mental health 141.32-3
    racial equality 118.13-16
    and violence 118.7, 8
    wages 118.11
forced labour 167.20, 22
forced marriages 155.16-18; 166.17-20
    children 167.32
foreign-born population
    UK 150.29, 30
    worldwide 150.33
foreign investment 157.37
foreign students and terrorism 147.13-14
forests
    and carbon sequestration 151.26
    effect of increased trade 157.14
    and sustainability 146.30-31
    threatened species of animals in 78.1, 2, 5

G

climate change accord **151**.16-17
  protests **121**.14
gambling **129**.1-39
  addiction *see* compulsive gambling
  addictiveness **129**.30
  benefits **129**.18
  controlled **129**.2, 28
  definition **129**.1, 28
  effects **129**.36
    physical **129**.29, 36
    psychological **129**.6, 29
    research **129**.16
  expenditure on **129**.4
    children **129**.32, 33
    mobile gambling **129**.26
    National Lottery **129**.9, 10
    online gambling **129**.17, 19
  forms of **129**.2
  history of **129**.1
  and law
    Gambling Act **129**.5, 17, 23
    and gambling at work **129**.23
    online gambling **129**.17
  licensing **129**.5, 8, 23
  by mobiles **129**.18, 26
  and neurobiology **129**.6
  online gambling **129**.17-18, 19-25
  participation in **129**.4
    National Lottery **129**.9, 10
    online gambling **129**.19
    young people **129**.11
  problem gamblers *see* compulsive gambling
  psychology of **129**.6, 29
  signs of problems **129**.22-3, 24, 28, 29, 35-6, 38
  social factors **129**.7, 29
  statistics **129**.1-3, 4
  underage **129**.1
    National Lottery **129**.11-13
    online gambling **129**.18, 25
    online poker **129**.25
    Scotland **129**.32-3
  at work **129**.22-4
  women **129**.21, 27, 34
  young people **129**.1
    addiction **129**.25, 31, 32-3
    National Lottery **129**.11-13
    signs of gambling problems **129**.38
    views on gambling **129**.13
  see also casinos; compulsive gambling; National Lottery
gamete donation *see* egg donation; sperm donation
gamete intrafallopian transfer (GIFT) **178**.11
gamete market **178**.12
gaming
  addiction to **158**.39
  concerns about violence **158**.33
gangs **177**.9-10, 12-14
  dealing with **177**.9-10, 14
  definition **177**.10
  signs of membership **177**.12-13
gap years **107**.27; **156**.15-19
gardens and water conservation **76**.1, 36, 37, 38

garment companies, working conditions **157**.27-9
gastric surgery for weight loss **162**.3
gateway effect, cannabis use **128**.9-10, 11, 28
gay adoption **153**.31-2
gay couples
  adoption and fostering **153**.34
  fertility treatment **153**.33-4
  having a child **153**.20-22; **178**.9-10
gay gene theory **153**.6
gay issues in children's literature **153**.19-20
gay men
  in boardroom positions **153**.39
  and depression **125**.15
  and HIV **96**.17, 20, 23; **164**.22
    HIV prevention campaigns **164**.24
    infection rate **164**.16, 17, 22
    life expectancy **164**.9
  and the media **142**.39
  and sexually transmitted infections (STIs) **96**.3, 4, 10, 12
  see also homosexuality
GCSEs **139**.4
  academies **139**.14, 15
  and ethnicity **139**.8
  gender differences **154**.22
  results **139**.2
GDP (Gross Domestic Product) **157**.6
  as measure of living standards **157**.13
gender
  and alcohol consumption **143**.16, 31
  and alcohol effects **143**.7
  and alcohol limits **143**.27
  and Alzheimer's disease **159**.36
  and attitudes to sex **173**.12-13
  and cannabis use **128**.22
  and car use **119**.29
  and child pedestrian accidents **119**.5
  of children and effects of divorce **124**.33
  and compulsive shopping **134**.14
  definition **154**.1
  and depression **125**.2
  development **154**.1
  differences **154**.1, 9
  and disability **135**.2
  and drug abuse **163**.29-30
  and education *see* gender and education
  homeless people **130**.10, 14
  and household financial roles **180**.18-19
  and mental ill-health **141**.1
  and online shopping **134**.16
  and pay *see* gender pay gap
  and schizophrenia **141**.4
  and self-harm **136**.7, 24, 26
  and smoking **145**.1, 21, 22
    children **145**.2, 5
  and society **154**.1-14
  and stress **100**.13, 19
  and suicide risk **136**.33
  and work **154**.29-35
  see also gender pay gap; men; women
gender-based violence **154**.12
  see also domestic abuse; rape

gender and education **139**.10-11; **154**.22-7
   A-level performance **139**.18
   and educational performance **139**.2; **154**.22, 23
   higher education **139**.32
   reasons for gender gap **154**.25
   subject choices **139**.11; **154**.26
   worldwide **154**.12
gender equality
   changes since 1970s **154**.5
   goals **154**.2-4, 6
   Millennium Development Goals **160**.13
gender equity in sport **118**.18-19
gender inequality **154**.2-4
   and HIV **164**.5-6
   worldwide **154**.12-14
gender pay gap **107**.13, 25, 26; **154**.2-3, 6, 30, 35-9
   graduates **139**.36
   senior management **154**.38
gender power gap **154**.4, 6
gender-specific behaviour **154**.1, 9
gender stereotypes
   and bullying **165**.12-13
   in careers advice **154**.28
   male **154**.7-8
gender and work **154**.29-35
   careers advice **154**.28, 35
   and pay *see* gender pay gap
   see also women in the workforce
general practitioners *see* GPs (general practitioners)
gene doping **118**.34
gene therapy **118**.39
General Elections **131**.18
genes **138**.4, 12; **178**.3
   and addiction **141**.9
   and ageing **159**.2, 32
   and Alzheimer's disease **159**.36
   and attention-deficit hyperactivity disorder (ADHD) **141**.19
   and depression **125**.2
   and eating disorders **127**.6-7
   and obesity **127**.35; **162**.9-10
   and sexuality **153**.6, 7
genetic barriers **144**.12

genetic biodiversity **146**.18
genetic engineering **144**.20
genetic modification
   definition **138**.1, 2, 4
   and the environment **138**.12-14, 24
   ethical issues **138**.23
   limitations **138**.37-8
   product labeling **138**.11, 25, 39
   public attitudes to **138**.3, 15-16
   technologies **138**.35
genetically modified animals, experiments on **144**.34; **169**.16, 17
genetically modified (GM) crops **88**.14, 32, 33; **146**.26-7
   and animal feed **138**.25
   benefits of **138**.8-10
   crop area **138**.2, 25, 29
   cross-contamination **138**.6-7, 12-13
   developing countries **138**.9, 10, 23, 29-30, 34-5
   drug crops (pharming) **138**.4, 9-10, 20-22
   and food production **140**.37
   future for **138**.13; **146**.26-7
   land register proposal **138**.36
   non-food crops **138**.10, 14
   potato research trials **138**.27, 28
   rice **138**.20, 31-4
   risks **138**.8-10, 24
   safety **138**.6
   tobacco plants **138**.21-2
   UK **138**.2-3, 5, 39
genetically modified organisms (GMOs)
   benefits **138**.12
   concerns about **138**.12-13, 24
   definition **138**.4, 12
   hens **138**.20-21
   see also genetically modified crops
genital herpes **173**.18, 21
genital warts **173**.18, 20-21
Genito-Urinary Medicine (GUM) clinics **96**.1, 10
   health advisers and safer sex **96**.1, 10
   and HIV testing **96**.16
   pressure on services **96**.3, 4, 8-9, 11
   tests and treatment offered at **96**.10

Volume numbers appear first (in bold) followed by page numbers; a change in volume number is preceded by a semi-colon.

Vol. 76 The Water Crisis
Vol. 78 Threatened Species
Vol. 81 Alternative Therapies
Vol. 88 Food and Nutrition
Vol. 89 Refugees
Vol. 97 Energy Matters
Vol. 99 Exploited Children
Vol. 100 Stress and Anxiety
Vol. 107 Work Issues
Vol. 116 Grief and Loss
Vol. 118 Focus on Sport
Vol. 119 Transport Trends
Vol. 121 The Censorship Debate
Vol. 124 Parenting Issues
Vol. 125 Understanding Depression
Vol. 127 Eating Disorders
Vol. 128 The Cannabis Issue
Vol. 129 Gambling Trends
Vol. 130 Homelessness
Vol. 133 Teen Pregnancy and Lone Parents
Vol. 134 Customers and Consumerism
Vol. 135 Coping with Disability
Vol. 136 Self-Harm

Vol. 138 A Genetically Modified Future?
Vol. 139 The Education Problem
Vol. 140 Vegetarian and Vegan Diets
Vol. 141 Mental Health
Vol. 142 Media Issues
Vol. 143 Problem Drinking
Vol. 144 The Cloning Debate
Vol. 145 Smoking Trends
Vol. 146 Sustainability and Environment
Vol. 147 The Terrorism Problem
Vol. 148 Religious Beliefs
Vol. 149 A Classless Society?
Vol. 150 Migration and Population
Vol. 151 Climate Change
Vol. 152 Euthanasia and the Right to Die
Vol. 153 Sexual Orientation and Society
Vol. 154 The Gender Gap
Vol. 155 Domestic Abuse
Vol. 156 Travel and Tourism
Vol. 157 The Problem of Globalisation
Vol. 158 The Internet Revolution
Vol. 159 An Ageing Population
Vol. 160 Poverty and Exclusion

Vol. 161 Waste Issues
Vol. 162 Staying Fit
Vol. 163 Drugs in the UK
Vol. 164 The AIDS Crisis
Vol. 165 Bullying Issues
Vol. 166 Marriage and Cohabitation
Vol. 167 Our Human Rights
Vol. 168 Privacy and Surveillance
Vol. 169 The Animal Rights Debate
Vol. 170 Body Image and Self-Esteem
Vol. 171 Abortion – Rights and Ethics
Vol. 172 Racial and Ethnic Discrimination
Vol. 173 Sexual Health
Vol. 174 Selling Sex
Vol. 175 Citizenship and Participation
Vol. 176 Health Issues for Young People
Vol. 177 Crime in the UK
Vol. 178 Reproductive Ethics
Vol. 179 Tackling Child Abuse
Vol. 180 Money and Finances
Vol. 181 The Housing Issue

genomics **138**.2-3, 37-9
geothermal energy **97**.6-7, 9, 11-12
germ line therapy **144**.20
germ line transmission **144**.26
germs **88**.27, 28-9
gestational surrogacy **178**.7, 13
ghettos **115**.28, 31
gifted and talented scheme, and black pupils **139**.9
girls' schools **154**.27
girls and young women
    attitudes to sex **173**.12-13
    and beauty salons **170**.25-6
    and body image **170**.21-2, 24
    careers information **154**.28, 35
    and child labour **99**.2, 3
    child soldiers **99**.29, 31, 36
    and cosmetic surgery **170**.32-3
    discrimination against **154**.13-14
    drug abuse **163**.29-30
    and education **154**.22-6
        examination results **154**.22, 23
        foundation stage **154**.23
        single-sex education **154**.27
        subject choices **154**.22, 26
    and mental health problems **141**.1
    and puberty **127**.22
    and self-harm **136**.7
    sexual exploitation of **99**.16, 20, 21-2
    sexualisation of **154**.10
    and smoking **145**.2, 5
    and sport **118**.20
    sport and self-esteem **170**.39
    street children **99**.18-19
    violence against **154**.13-14; **155**.26
glass ceiling **107**.9; **154**.38
    for homosexuals **153**.39
glass cliff **107**.9; **154**.34
global financial crisis **180**.1-2
Global Gag Rule **171**.13-14
global gender inequality **154**.12-14
global inequality **160**.26, 29
global interdependence **146**.4-6
global positioning system (GPS)
    and road charging **119**.36
    and surveillance
global poverty **160**.25-39
global trade, attitudes to **157**.39
global warming **151**.1
    and air travel **156**.26
    and biodiversity **146**.19
    causes of **151**.3-4, 5-6
    computer models **151**.5
    and consumer behaviour **134**.31
    costs **151**.8
    denial of **151**.14-15
    effects of **151**.1, 7, 8
    and energy efficiency **97**.29
    evidence for **151**.1, 3
    and renewable energy **97**.8
    see also climate change; energy efficiency; greenhouse gas
        emissions

globalization **157**.1-15
    benefits **157**.1, 25, 26-7
    and child labour **99**.14
    concerns about **157**.3, 9-11, 25, 37-8
    definition **157**.1, 2, 3, 6, 12
    and developing countries **157**.25
    and economic growth **157**.1
    effects of **157**.1, 3-4, 9-11, 12, 37-8
    and the environment **157**.10
    facts **157**.2
    and inequality **157**.3-4, 9
    monoculture fears **157**.11
    and multinationals **157**.30-31
    and trade **157**.17-39
    types **157**.2
GM crops *see* genetically modified (GM) crops
GMOs *see* genetically modified organisms
GNP (Gross National Product) **157**.6
GNVQs (General National Vocational Qualifications) **139**.4
Golden Rule **148**.8-9, 15-16
gonorrhoea **173**.18, 21
Google
    and Chinese censorship **121**.20-21
    Google Earth **168**.26-7
governance benefits of globalisation **157**.1
Government
    the Budget **180**.24
    control of the media **121**.1; **142**.2
    finance, and smoking **145**.1
    funding for higher education **180**.28, 33
    media censorship **121**.37
    media influence **142**.2
    Parliament **131**.15
    spending on aid **157**.10
    surveillance **168**.4-5, 7-8, 13-14, 27, 35
    use of the media **121**.17-18
Government policies
    on drugs **163**.22-4
    on genetically modified crops **138**.5
    on health **162**.4-5, 9-10, 17-18, 22-3
    on homelessness **130**.16, 28, 33
    on housing **181**.23
        missing affordable housing target **181**.6
        houses of multiple occupation **181**.19-20
        social housing **130**.16, 33
    on plastic bags **161**.14
    to reduce educational attainment gap **149**.30, 37-8
    sensible drinking guidelines *see* daily benchmarks on alcohol consumption
    on sexually transmitted infections **173**.21
    on smacking **179**.33
    waste strategy **161**.20
Government targets
    road safety **119**.4
governments
    role in globalisation **157**.4
    and the World Trade Organisation **157**.21
GPs (general practitioners)
    and abortions **171**.25-6
    and bereavement support **116**.2
    and complementary medicine **81**.21, 29, 34

and disability support **135**.4
and eating disorders **127**.28
registering at university **176**.5
reporting a death **116**.31
seeking help for stress from **100**.2, 33, 34
see also doctors
GPS *see* global positioning system
graduates **107**.14-15, 35-6
basic skills concerns **139**.17
debt **139**.35
earnings **139**.35, 36, 37
employment **139**.33
and social class **149**.2
incentives for teacher training **139**.12
starting salaries **139**.35, 36
unemployment **180**.35
grandparents
and childcare **124**.1, 37-8
opinions of parenting skills **124**.2
grants, student **139**.34; **180**.28, 33
graves **116**.37
visiting **116**.16
green belt land **181**.21, 36
green burials **116**.39
green cars *see* fuel efficient cars
green consumerism **146**.38-9
green infrastructure **181**.36
green space and mental health **141**.35
green waste **161**.28-9, 30
greenfield development **181**.22, 36
greenhouse effect **151**.1, 3
greenhouse gases **151**.1, 7
emission reduction targets **146**.8-9
emissions, China **146**.5
emissions from tourism **156**.25
sequestration **151**.26
see also carbon dioxide emissions
greenwashing **156**.24
grief **116**.1-2, 3-5, 7-9
counselling **116**.6
importance of grieving **116**.3
length of grieving process **116**.4-5

public **116**.17-18
and traumatic bereavement **116**.10-11
and young people **116**.19-28
grooming, online **179**.16
Gross Domestic Product (GDP) **157**.6
Gross National Product (GNP) **157**.6
guarantees, consumer rights **134**.18-19
guilt, feelings after bereavement **116**.4, 11, 19
children **116**.27
and traumatic bereavement **116**.11
gun crime **177**.15-16, 29-30
young people's concerns **177**.15-16
guns and the law **177**.7
GURTs (Genetic Use Restriction Technologies) **138**.18
gym drugs **118**.35
Gypsy/Roma children and education **115**.18

H

habitat loss
and endangered wildlife in Britain **78**.30-1, 32
haematopoietic cell transplantation (HTD) **144**.21
haemophiliacs and HIV **164**.25
hair, stem cell therapy **144**.22
hallucinogens (psychedelics) **163**.2, 6
hangovers and exercise **162**.32
happiness
of children, effect of paretnal relationship **166**.32
in marriage **166**.7-8
teaching in schools **170**.14-15
happy slapping **165**.31
haram foods, Islam **148**.11
harassment
racial **115**.8
on grounds of sexual orientation **153**.38
hard segregation **115**.28
hashish (cannabis resins) **128**.1, 3, 6, 23
hazardous waste **161**.6, 32
hazardous work
and child labour **99**.1, 2, 3
domestic labour **99**.7

Volume numbers appear first (in bold) followed by page numbers; a change in volume number is preceded by a semi-colon.

Vol. 76 The Water Crisis	**Vol. 138** A Genetically Modified Future?	**Vol. 161** Waste Issues
Vol. 78 Threatened Species	**Vol. 139** The Education Problem	**Vol. 162** Staying Fit
Vol. 81 Alternative Therapies	**Vol. 140** Vegetarian and Vegan Diets	**Vol. 163** Drugs in the UK
Vol. 88 Food and Nutrition	**Vol. 141** Mental Health	**Vol. 164** The AIDS Crisis
Vol. 89 Refugees	**Vol. 142** Media Issues	**Vol. 165** Bullying Issues
Vol. 97 Energy Matters	**Vol. 143** Problem Drinking	**Vol. 166** Marriage and Cohabitation
Vol. 99 Exploited Children	**Vol. 144** The Cloning Debate	**Vol. 167** Our Human Rights
Vol. 100 Stress and Anxiety	**Vol. 145** Smoking Trends	**Vol. 168** Privacy and Surveillance
Vol. 107 Work Issues	**Vol. 146** Sustainability and Environment	**Vol. 169** The Animal Rights Debate
Vol. 116 Grief and Loss	**Vol. 147** The Terrorism Problem	**Vol. 170** Body Image and Self-Esteem
Vol. 118 Focus on Sport	**Vol. 148** Religious Beliefs	**Vol. 171** Abortion – Rights and Ethics
Vol. 119 Transport Trends	**Vol. 149** A Classless Society?	**Vol. 172** Racial and Ethnic Discrimination
Vol. 121 The Censorship Debate	**Vol. 150** Migration and Population	**Vol. 173** Sexual Health
Vol. 124 Parenting Issues	**Vol. 151** Climate Change	**Vol. 174** Selling Sex
Vol. 125 Understanding Depression	**Vol. 152** Euthanasia and the Right to Die	**Vol. 175** Citizenship and Participation
Vol. 127 Eating Disorders	**Vol. 153** Sexual Orientation and Society	**Vol. 176** Health Issues for Young People
Vol. 128 The Cannabis Issue	**Vol. 154** The Gender Gap	**Vol. 177** Crime in the UK
Vol. 129 Gambling Trends	**Vol. 155** Domestic Abuse	**Vol. 178** Reproductive Ethics
Vol. 130 Homelessness	**Vol. 156** Travel and Tourism	**Vol. 179** Tackling Child Abuse
Vol. 133 Teen Pregnancy and Lone Parents	**Vol. 157** The Problem of Globalisation	**Vol. 180** Money and Finances
Vol. 134 Customers and Consumerism	**Vol. 158** The Internet Revolution	**Vol. 181** The Housing Issue
Vol. 135 Coping with Disability	**Vol. 159** An Ageing Population	
Vol. 136 Self-Harm	**Vol. 160** Poverty and Exclusion	

head injuries and risk of Alzheimer's disease **159**.36
headteachers, gender gap **154**.25
health **176**.1-39
   and alcohol **143**.4, 6, 7, 9-10, 27
   and body image **170**.23, 38
   and cannabis **163**.6, 9, 35
      and the immune system **128**.19
      and lung cancer **128**.17, 19, 28
      respiratory effects **128**.18-19
      reclassification of **128**.30-32, 38
   census information **150**.36
   and cloning **144**.2, 6, 39
   and compulsive exercise **162**.39
   and cycling **119**.39
   and drugs
      amphetamines **163**.4-5
      cocaine **163**.4
      ecstasy **163**.5, 10
      LSD **163**.6
      opiates **163**.5
      solvents **163**.6
   and eating disorders **127**.4-5
   gender gap **154**.6
   and GM crops **138**.9-10
      see also pharming
   government strategies **162**.4-5, 9-10, 17-18, 22-3
   holidays **156**.4-5
   and homeless people **130**.20
      children **130**.23
      older people **130**.17
   and marital status **166**.15
   and meat consumption **140**.12, 13, 21
   and migrants **150**.21-3
   and obesity **127**.32, 34; **162**.1-2, 5, 6, 7, 19, 25
   older people **159**.4, 6, 8, 34
   and physical activity **118**.3, 20
   and poverty **160**.2
   and smoking **145**.25-39
      benefits of giving up **145**.27, 35
      children **145**.2
      developing countries **145**.23
      passive smoking **145**.2, 28-9
      and smoking ban **145**.12
   and social class **149**.13-14
   students **176**.5-6
   and traffic increase **119**.1
   and traffic pollution **119**.13-14, 31
   and vegetarian diets **140**.1, 2-3, 5, 11
   and walking to school **119**.27, 31
   young carers **141**.24
   see also mental health; mental illness; sexual health
health care
   costs, obesity **127**.33-4, 37
   and disabled people **135**.4; 20
   effect of legalizing euthanasia **152**.4
   older people **159**.6
      see also care services for older people
   and refugees **89**.19-20
   UK dependence on workers from overseas **146**.6
health education on smoking **145**.3, 5; **176**.13
health and safety issues, WTO **157**.23

health warnings on alcohol **143**.30, 31, 32
health and wellness holidays **156**.4-5
healthy eating **88**.1-2, 5-7; **127**.23
   children **162**.25-6; **176**.3
   as help for depression **125**.3, 39
   government strategies **162**.10, 17-18
   and meat consumption **140**.12, 14, 21
   and social class **162**.13-14
   and stress relief **100**.30, 31, 34, 35, 38-9
   tyranny **162**.16
   and vegetarian diets **140**.1, 3-4, , 6, 7, 10, 11
   young people **176**.3, 8-9
   see also diet; food and nutrition
hearing, stem cell therapy **144**.22
heart attacks and cycling **119**.39
heart disease
   and depression **125**.5
   and eating disorders **127**.5
   and obesity **162**.7
   protective effect of alcohol **143**.7, 27
   stem cell therapy **144**.22, 23, 28
   and stress **100**.19
heatstroke and ecstasy **163**.10
heavy drinking **143**.3, 8
   see also alcohol abuse
hemp **128**.6, 34
hepatitis **173**.18
herbal cannabis (marijuana/grass) **128**.2, 3, 6, 23
   seizures of **128**.31
   see also sinsemilla; skunk
herbal medicine **81**.4, 11, 23, 36
   banned herbs **81**.24
   Chinese **81**.14-15
   defining **81**.2, 11
   effectiveness of **81**.24
   expenditure on **81**.37
   and multiple sclerosis **81**.30
   and pharmaceutical drugs **81**.11
   regulation of **81**.23
   and scientists **81**.28, 29
heredity
   and Alzheimer's disease **159**.36
   and mental illness **141**.24
heroin **163**.5
   and cannabis use **128**.9-10
   market trends **163**.25
herpes *see* genital herpes
heterosexism **165**.13-14
heterosexual HIV infection rate **164**.16, 17
hidden homelessness **130**.3, 13, 21-2
high blood pressure (hypertension) **88**.2, 9, 16
   and depression **125**.5
higher education **139**.2, 29-39
   degree results **139**.33
   funding **139**.34; **180**.28, 33
   and social class **149**.1-2
   statistics **139**.32
   see also further education; graduates; students; universities
Highers (exams) **139**.4
Hinduism **148**.2-3
   and faith schools **148**.35-6

festivals **148**.3

food rules **148**.3, 11

funerals **116**.34; **148**.3

hire purchase **134**.22; **180**.27

history, British, importance of teaching **131**.7

HIV (Human Immunodeficiency Virus) **164**.1-39

and anti-gay prejudice **153**.2

and child labour **99**.3

and child soldiers **99**.31

education **164**.18, 23-4

and migrant population **150**.22-3

Millennium Development Goals **160**.32

older people as carers **159**.5

and parents of lesbians and gay people **153**.9

and poverty **164**.10, 27

prevention **164**.3, 23-39

campaigns **164**.23-5

and condoms **164**.3

funding **164**.16, 39

targets **164**.28

worldwide access to prevention services **164**.39

and the sexual exploitation of children **99**.16, 24

signs and symptoms **164**.1-2

testing for **164**.2, 20-21

transmission **164**.1, 11

criminal **164**.12-13

mother-to-child **164**.3, 25, 27, 29-30, 31, 38

through blood products **164**.1, 19-20, 25

treatments **164**.2-3

antiretroviral therapy (ART) **164**.2-3, 8-9, 29, 30-32

combination therapy **164**.2-3, 8-9, 30-31

drugs from GM (pharmed) crops **138**.21, 22

side effects **164**.3, 31

vaccines **164**.34-6

worldwide access **164**.38-9

UK statistics **164**.16, 17, 22; **173**.3, 21

and women **164**.5-6

pregnant **164**.3, 25, 27, 29-30, 31

worldwide statistics **164**.4, 38-9

and young people **164**.18; **176**.4, 28

see also AIDS

holidays

and climate change concerns **156**.28-30

destinations **156**.3

as economic indicator **180**.5

ethical **134**.30

expenditure on **134**.3

as status symbols **156**.5

see also responsible tourism; tourism

Holocaust denial **121**.8, 12-13

home abortions **171**.35-6

home building **181**.2

affordable homes **181**.6, 29

green belt land **181**.21

greenfield sites **181**.22, 26

self-build **181**.30-31

home care services **159**.4

costs **159**.26

home expenditure, ethical **134**.32

home furnishings, spending on **134**.4

home information packs, political party policies **181**.23

home insulation **151**.38, 39

home learning **139**.27-8

home ownership

low-cost options **181**.25

pessimism about prospects **181**.5

and social class **149**.20

attitudes to moving home **149**.26

and social housing tenants **181**.33-5

young people **181**.26

home schooling **139**.27

home and sex education **133**.15

homeless households **130**.1

homeless young people **130**.14-15, 21-7

and debt **130**.24-6

hidden homelessness **130**.21-2

homelessness causes **130**.21

local authority duties **181**.26

mental health **130**.27

homelessness

and affordable housing **130**.8, 16, 23, 33

and beggars **130**.12

causes **130**.3, 6, 10-11

young people **130**.21

Volume numbers appear first (in bold) followed by page numbers; a change in volume number is preceded by a semi-colon.

Vol. 76 The Water Crisis

Vol. 78 Threatened Species

Vol. 81 Alternative Therapies

Vol. 88 Food and Nutrition

Vol. 89 Refugees

Vol. 97 Energy Matters

Vol. 99 Exploited Children

Vol. 100 Stress and Anxiety

Vol. 107 Work Issues

Vol. 116 Grief and Loss

Vol. 118 Focus on Sport

Vol. 119 Transport Trends

Vol. 121 The Censorship Debate

Vol. 124 Parenting Issues

Vol. 125 Understanding Depression

Vol. 127 Eating Disorders

Vol. 128 The Cannabis Issue

Vol. 129 Gambling Trends

Vol. 130 Homelessness

Vol. 133 Teen Pregnancy and Lone Parents

Vol. 134 Customers and Consumerism

Vol. 135 Coping with Disability

Vol. 136 Self-Harm

Vol. 138 A Genetically Modified Future?

Vol. 139 The Education Problem

Vol. 140 Vegetarian and Vegan Diets

Vol. 141 Mental Health

Vol. 142 Media Issues

Vol. 143 Problem Drinking

Vol. 144 The Cloning Debate

Vol. 145 Smoking Trends

Vol. 146 Sustainability and Environment

Vol. 147 The Terrorism Problem

Vol. 148 Religious Beliefs

Vol. 149 A Classless Society?

Vol. 150 Migration and Population

Vol. 151 Climate Change

Vol. 152 Euthanasia and the Right to Die

Vol. 153 Sexual Orientation and Society

Vol. 154 The Gender Gap

Vol. 155 Domestic Abuse

Vol. 156 Travel and Tourism

Vol. 157 The Problem of Globalisation

Vol. 158 The Internet Revolution

Vol. 159 An Ageing Population

Vol. 160 Poverty and Exclusion

Vol. 161 Waste Issues

Vol. 162 Staying Fit

Vol. 163 Drugs in the UK

Vol. 164 The AIDS Crisis

Vol. 165 Bullying Issues

Vol. 166 Marriage and Cohabitation

Vol. 167 Our Human Rights

Vol. 168 Privacy and Surveillance

Vol. 169 The Animal Rights Debate

Vol. 170 Body Image and Self-Esteem

Vol. 171 Abortion – Rights and Ethics

Vol. 172 Racial and Ethnic Discrimination

Vol. 173 Sexual Health

Vol. 174 Selling Sex

Vol. 175 Citizenship and Participation

Vol. 176 Health Issues for Young People

Vol. 177 Crime in the UK

Vol. 178 Reproductive Ethics

Vol. 179 Tackling Child Abuse

Vol. 180 Money and Finances

Vol. 181 The Housing Issue

and children 130.23
defining 130.1-3
and drug use 130.11, 20
and employment 130.15, 36-7
and health 130.20
   children 130.23
   older people 130.17
government strategies 130.16, 28, 33
help for homeless people 130.21-2, 28-39
hidden homeless 130.3, 13, 21-2
history of 130.4
intentionally homeless 130.2
and local authorities 130.2-3, 28, 29-30
and mental health problems 130.20
   street homeless 130.11
   young people 130.27
myths and facts 130.7
and older people 130.17-18; 159.4
preventing 130.28-30
priority needs homeless 130.2
reduction in 130.16
repeat homelessness 130.34
risk factors 130.3
rough sleeping 130.6, 9-12
statistics 130.13-15, 22
see also homeless young people; street homelessness;
   temporary accommodation
homeopathy 81.12-13, 23, 36
and cancer 81.32
defining 81.2, 12
effectiveness of 81.22, 24, 28
expenditure on 81.37
and the placebo effect 81.26
and scientists 81.28-9
treatments 81.12-13
homework 139.27, 28
homeworking 107.12, 14-15, 19-20, 22
scams 134.27
homophobia 153.13
in football 118.17
homophobic abuse 165.13
homophobic bullying 153.14-18; 165.2, 9, 12-14
homosexuality 153.1-3
causes 153.3, 6, 7
coming out 153.3, 8
'correction' of 153.3
discrimination 153.2-3, 27-8
genetic factors 153.6, 7
and the media 142.39; 153.23-5
and mental disorder 153.3, 4
and young people 133.2
see also gay men; lesbians
hooliganism, football 118.7, 8
hormones
and appetite regulation 127.38-9
use in sport 118.37
hospitals
admission for manic depression 125.19-20
admission for self-harm 136.4, 10
death, formal procedures 116.31
host surrogacy 178.7, 13

hostels 130.31
hot water bottles, recycling 161.24-5
hotels, limiting environmental impact 156.24
hours of work 107.2, 3, 6, 14, 24
   fathers 124.11
   full-time mothers 124.12
   see also employment
House of Commons 131.15
House of Lords 131.15
house prices 134.25
   and homelessness 130.8
house size, new homes 181.15
household crime, racial identity of victims 115.10
household debt 180.9
household tasks and working parents 124.11
household waste 161.1, 5, 6, 18-19, 31
   composition of 161.1
   see also composting waste; waste management
households
   and energy efficiency 97.2, 27-30, 31, 32-3; 151.39
   gender roles 154.15, 21
      financial 180.18-19
   growth in numbers of 181.2
   income inequalities 160.6-7
   minimum standard income 160.8; 180.6
   structure and poverty 160.2
   see also families; homeless households
houses of multiple occupation 181.19-20
housework
   and gender 154.15
   parents, time spent on 124.11
housing 181.1-39
   advice centres 130.29
   census information 150.36
   and children 181.9-11, 13, 14
   debt 134.23
   expenditure 134.4
   home building 181.2
      affordable homes 181.6, 29
      green belt land 181.21
      greenfield sites 181.22, 36
      self-build 181.30-31
   housing market as economic indicator 180.5
   and lone parents 133.37
   new homes
      lack of space 181.15
      need for 181.6,29
      political party policies 181.23
   older people 159.4
   overcrowding 181.14
   problems for young people 180.35-6
   rented accommodation shortage 130.8
   shortage 130.8, 16, 30
   size of new houses 181.15
   social housing *see* social housing
   and social improvement 181.33-5
   young people 180.35-6
   see also affordable housing; home ownership; homelessness;
      rural housing; temporary accommodation
housing associations
   and self-build projects 181.30, 31

and tenants' rights to move 181.35-6
Housing Benefit 133.34-5; 135.5
    problems, and homelessness 130.9
human-animal embryos 144.9, 11, 13, 14, 20; 178.35
human-ape hybrids 144.11
human cloning 144.1-14
    ethical issues 144.2-3, 5-6, 7-8
    public attitudes 144.35
human dignity
    and cloning 144.3
    and inter-species mixing 144.12
human embryos
    stem cells see embryonic stem cells
    hybrid embryos 144.9, 11, 13, 14, 20
Human Fertilisation and Embryology Act 144.15, 27; 171.5, 7
human genes
    in bacteria 144.11
    in mice 144.11
    see also hybrid embryos
human growth hormones (HGHs) and sport 118.37
human reproductive cloning
    autonomy issues 144.3
    benefits 144.2
    and dignity 144.3
    ethical concerns 144.2-3, 8
human rights 167.1-27
    and cartoons of Mohammed 121.11-12
    and child labour 99.4, 6
        domestic work 99.8
    and child soldiers 99.30, 31-2
    and children's rights 167.28-39
    controversies 167.5
    and corporal punishment 179.30, 31-2
    definitions 167.1, 4
    development of 167.1, 6-7
    female migrants 150.15
    laws 167.2
        see also Human Rights Act
    and politics 167.4-5
    and privacy 168.1, 3
    public attitudes to 167.19
    smoking ban challenge 145.15
    timeline 167.6-7
    water as a human right 76.24-5, 32
Human Rights, Universal Declaration of 167.8-10, 14
    and privacy 168.3
Human Rights Act 167.3, 4, 5, 15-18
    achievements 167.17-18
    costs 167.18
    failures 167.16-17
humanism
    and abortion 171.19-21
    and animal welfare 140.31-3
    and embryo research 144.7-8; 178.36-7
    and ethics 148.13-16
    funerals 116.35
    and the Golden Rule 148.8, 15-16
    motivation 148.14
humidity, global increase 151.2
hunger 160.28
    Millennium Development Goals 160.30
hunger strikers, force-feeding 167.26
hunting 169.27-36
    after the ban 169.34-5
    arguments against 169.27, 30-33, 33
    arguments for 169.27
    for bushmeat 78.18
    draghunting 169.33
    as food source 140.17
    hunt monitors 169.35
    hunting with dogs 169.27-36
    increased popularity since ban 169.34-5
    law on (Hunting Act 2004) 169.28-9, 30-32
    and mammals in the UK 78.32
    public attitudes to 169.29, 36
    trail hunting 169.34
    whales 78.6, 13, 14
    of wildlife 78.2, 4-5, 5-6
hybrid animals 144.10-12
hybrid embryos 144.9, 11, 13, 14, 20
hybrid vehicles 119.22
hybridisation 138.12-13
    see also cross-contamination; cross-pollination
hydrocarbon (HC) emissions 119.15

Volume numbers appear first (in bold) followed by page numbers; a change in volume number is preceded by a semi-colon.

Vol. 76 The Water Crisis
Vol. 78 Threatened Species
Vol. 81 Alternative Therapies
Vol. 88 Food and Nutrition
Vol. 89 Refugees
Vol. 97 Energy Matters
Vol. 99 Exploited Children
Vol. 100 Stress and Anxiety
Vol. 107 Work Issues
Vol. 116 Grief and Loss
Vol. 118 Focus on Sport
Vol. 119 Transport Trends
Vol. 121 The Censorship Debate
Vol. 124 Parenting Issues
Vol. 125 Understanding Depression
Vol. 127 Eating Disorders
Vol. 128 The Cannabis Issue
Vol. 129 Gambling Trends
Vol. 130 Homelessness
Vol. 133 Teen Pregnancy and Lone Parents
Vol. 134 Customers and Consumerism
Vol. 135 Coping with Disability
Vol. 136 Self-Harm

Vol. 138 A Genetically Modified Future?
Vol. 139 The Education Problem
Vol. 140 Vegetarian and Vegan Diets
Vol. 141 Mental Health
Vol. 142 Media Issues
Vol. 143 Problem Drinking
Vol. 144 The Cloning Debate
Vol. 145 Smoking Trends
Vol. 146 Sustainability and Environment
Vol. 147 The Terrorism Problem
Vol. 148 Religious Beliefs
Vol. 149 A Classless Society?
Vol. 150 Migration and Population
Vol. 151 Climate Change
Vol. 152 Euthanasia and the Right to Die
Vol. 153 Sexual Orientation and Society
Vol. 154 The Gender Gap
Vol. 155 Domestic Abuse
Vol. 156 Travel and Tourism
Vol. 157 The Problem of Globalisation
Vol. 158 The Internet Revolution
Vol. 159 An Ageing Population
Vol. 160 Poverty and Exclusion

Vol. 161 Waste Issues
Vol. 162 Staying Fit
Vol. 163 Drugs in the UK
Vol. 164 The AIDS Crisis
Vol. 165 Bullying Issues
Vol. 166 Marriage and Cohabitation
Vol. 167 Our Human Rights
Vol. 168 Privacy and Surveillance
Vol. 169 The Animal Rights Debate
Vol. 170 Body Image and Self-Esteem
Vol. 171 Abortion – Rights and Ethics
Vol. 172 Racial and Ethnic Discrimination
Vol. 173 Sexual Health
Vol. 174 Selling Sex
Vol. 175 Citizenship and Participation
Vol. 176 Health Issues for Young People
Vol. 177 Crime in the UK
Vol. 178 Reproductive Ethics
Vol. 179 Tackling Child Abuse
Vol. 180 Money and Finances
Vol. 181 The Housing Issue

I

ICSI (intracytoplasmic sperm injection) 178.8
identity
    British identity of non-white ethnic groups 115.38
    identity confusion 149.4-5
    protection in interviews 142.12
    protection online 158.10
    racial, victims of crime 115.10
    religious 115.5, 26
    and social class 149.3, 4, 18, 19, 24
    social identity and football supporters 141.32-3
identity (ID) cards 131.13-14; 168.14-19
    benefits 168.14-16
    costs 168.17, 18-19
    problems 168.17-19
    public attitudes to 168.16
identity disorders 141.11
identity fraud 134.27-8, 28-9; 158.3, 32, 33-4
    and ID cards 168.14-15, 18
    statistics 168.15-16
illegal broadcasting 142.7
illegal dumping *see* fly-tipping
illegal employment 89.10-11, 30-1
illegal immigrants 89.11, 30-1
    attitudes to 150.3
    and National Identity Scheme 168.16, 18
illegal parking 119.9
illegal planting of GM crops 138.19
illegal wildlife trade souvenirs 156.32
illness
    and depression 125.2, 5-6
    as reason for not exercising 162.31
images, effects on young people's behaviour 145.6
IMF (International Monetary Fund) 157.6, 10, 17
immigration
    attitudes to 150.3, 13-14, 17, 18-19
    church attendance of immigrants 148.23-4
    definition 150.21
    illegal immigrants 89.11, 30-1
    lack of accurate data 150.19
    and globalisation 157.37
    and population growth, UK 150.16
    problems of 150.16-17
    quota system proposal 131.10
    and social housing 181.12
    statistics, UK 150.4, 8-9
    worldwide 150.33
    see also asylum seekers; ethnic minorities; migrant workers;
      migrants
immune system
    effect of cannabis 128.19
    and HIV 164.1
imports
    UK dependence on 146.4-6
in vitro fertilisation (IVF) 178.1, 5-8, 11
    errors 178.22
    ethical dilemmas 178.17
    international comparisons 178.8
    and multiple births 178.6-7, 21-2
    and older mothers 178.17, 19-20
    statistics 178.5-6
    tagging embryos 178.22-3
    travelling abroad for 178.18, 20
inactivity
    children 162.13, 15, 25
    health effects 162.11
incentives
    for reducing waste 161.38
    for weight loss 162.22-3
incineration of waste 161.7
incitement to religious hatred 148.29
inclusion
    and sport 118.12
      disabled people 118.22
      ethnic minorities 118.13-16
      women 118.18-22
inclusive education 135.37-9
Income Support 133.33; 135.5
incomes 107.2, 13
    and children's educational attainment 149.25
    global 157.2
    inequalities 160.6, 7
      see also rich-poor gap
    lone-parent families 124.35; 133.28, 30
    minimum standard 160.8; 180.6
    minimum wage 107.31
    and part-time working 107.17
    pensioners 159.3
    and social class 149.19, 20
    social housing tenants 181.35
    stress and income levels 100.13
    and voter turnout 131.19
    see also earnings; gender pay gap; salaries; wages
incontinence
    sufferers 159.4
    and stem cell therapy 144.21
independence, encouraging children's 124.13-14
independent living and learning disabilities 135.34-5
independent schools and SEN provision 135.36
indirect discrimination
    racial 115.7, 11
    on sexuality 153.38
induced pluripotent stem cells (iPS cells) 178.38
Industrial Revolution and sport 118.24
industry
    and child labour 99.1, 2
    motivations for GM development 138.8
    water consumption 76.2, 8, 36
    water pollution 76.11
inequality
    attitudes to 160.9
    children 167.35
    in climate change effects 151.11, 19
    effect of free trade 157.13, 23-4
    gender *see* gender gap
    global 160.26, 28
    and globalisation 157.2, 3-4, 9
    of incomes 160.6, 7
    and segregation 115.30, 31, 32
    and tourism 156.20

infections
    as cause of anorexia 127.12
    as cause of depression 125.5
infertility 178.2-5
information
    as consumer right 134.1-2
    for disabled children 135.21
    and ethical consumerism 134.33-4
    personal, control of 158.31-4; 168.10-11, 31-2, 37
    privacy 168.2
    and the web 158.2
    see also Freedom of Information Act
information technology (IT)
    benefits 157.1
    and globalisation 157.1, 2, 15
    see also computers
inheritance and cohabitation 166.15
inherited learning disability 135.33
injury as reason for not exercising 162.32
injuries
    from domestic violence 155.30
    young people 176.4
inner city areas, voter turnout 131.19
inquests 116.32
insects, GM viral infections 138.13-14
insecurity
    feelings after bereavement 116.4
insomnia
    and stress 100.19, 29
instant messaging (IM) and bullying 165.24
institutional elements of marriage 166.2-3
institutions, leaving, as cause of homelessness 130.11
instructions to discriminate 115.12
insulation, home 151.38, 39
insulin, effect of nicotine 145.26
insurance
    car insurance offences 119.9
    and home buying 181.24
    and homeworking 107.20
integrated medicine/healthcare 81.36-8
integration, racial see racial integration
intellectual property rights see patents

intelligent design 148.37-9
intelligent transport systems 119.38
intensive farming
    arguments for 169.11-12
    chickens 169.13
    see also battery eggs
intentionally homeless people 130.2
interactive gambling 129.17-26
interdependence, global 146.4-6
interest free credit 134.22
interest-only mortgages 181.28
interest rates
    annual percentage rate (APR) 180.26
    as economic indicator 180.5
inter-ethnic marriages 115.25
    see also mixed-race relationships
interfaith relations, young people 148.32-3
intergender 153.13
internally displaced persons 89.1, 6, 8-9
international anti-doping policy 118.27-8, 31-2
international companies see multinational corporations
International Monetary Fund (IMF) see IMF
international parental chid abduction 166.36
international students 139.30, 31, 32
    and terrorism 147.13-14
international terrorism, history of 147.4-5
international trade 157.17-39
    ecologically wasteful 146.5
    facts 157.19
    and genetic modification 138.27
    and poverty 157.26-7; 160.37-8
    and taxes 157.12-13
    UK dependence on 146.4-6
    see also free trade; globalisation
Internet
    abortion drugs availability 171.35-6
    addiction 142.37; 158.38-9
    advertising 158.5
    anti-extremism projects 147.34
    banking 180.14
    broadband access 158.5-6, 17, 18
    bullying by e-mail 165.23-4, 38-9

Volume numbers appear first (in bold) followed by page numbers; a change in volume number is preceded by a semi-colon.

Vol. 76 The Water Crisis
Vol. 78 Threatened Species
Vol. 81 Alternative Therapies
Vol. 88 Food and Nutrition
Vol. 89 Refugees
Vol. 97 Energy Matters
Vol. 99 Exploited Children
Vol. 100 Stress and Anxiety
Vol. 107 Work Issues
Vol. 116 Grief and Loss
Vol. 118 Focus on Sport
Vol. 119 Transport Trends
Vol. 121 The Censorship Debate
Vol. 124 Parenting Issues
Vol. 125 Understanding Depression
Vol. 127 Eating Disorders
Vol. 128 The Cannabis Issue
Vol. 129 Gambling Trends
Vol. 130 Homelessness
Vol. 133 Teen Pregnancy and Lone Parents
Vol. 134 Customers and Consumerism
Vol. 135 Coping with Disability
Vol. 136 Self-Harm

Vol. 138 A Genetically Modified Future?
Vol. 139 The Education Problem
Vol. 140 Vegetarian and Vegan Diets
Vol. 141 Mental Health
Vol. 142 Media Issues
Vol. 143 Problem Drinking
Vol. 144 The Cloning Debate
Vol. 145 Smoking Trends
Vol. 146 Sustainability and Environment
Vol. 147 The Terrorism Problem
Vol. 148 Religious Beliefs
Vol. 149 A Classless Society?
Vol. 150 Migration and Population
Vol. 151 Climate Change
Vol. 152 Euthanasia and the Right to Die
Vol. 153 Sexual Orientation and Society
Vol. 154 The Gender Gap
Vol. 155 Domestic Abuse
Vol. 156 Travel and Tourism
Vol. 157 The Problem of Globalisation
Vol. 158 The Internet Revolution
Vol. 159 An Ageing Population
Vol. 160 Poverty and Exclusion

Vol. 161 Waste Issues
Vol. 162 Staying Fit
Vol. 163 Drugs in the UK
Vol. 164 The AIDS Crisis
Vol. 165 Bullying Issues
Vol. 166 Marriage and Cohabitation
Vol. 167 Our Human Rights
Vol. 168 Privacy and Surveillance
Vol. 169 The Animal Rights Debate
Vol. 170 Body Image and Self-Esteem
Vol. 171 Abortion – Rights and Ethics
Vol. 172 Racial and Ethnic Discrimination
Vol. 173 Sexual Health
Vol. 174 Selling Sex
Vol. 175 Citizenship and Participation
Vol. 176 Health Issues for Young People
Vol. 177 Crime in the UK
Vol. 178 Reproductive Ethics
Vol. 179 Tackling Child Abuse
Vol. 180 Money and Finances
Vol. 181 The Housing Issue

and censorship 121.18-21
and child sex abuse 179.15-17
and children and young people 158.20-21
development of 158.1
downloading 158.33, 35-6
and entertainment 158.21-2
family usage 158.7-8
filesharing 158.36
fraud 134.26-9
future of 158.25-6
gambling *see* online gambling
and globalisation 157.1, 2, 15
journalism register 142.16
and media regulation 142.2
National Lottery games, and under 16s 129.12-13
as news source 142.33
and newspapers 142.9
and older people 158.4
online activity 158.4, 15
  children 158.20-21
  older people 158.4
  young people 158.27
online bullying *see* cyberbullying
phishing 134.27-8, 28-9; 158.33-4
and privacy 168.34-6
reaching capacity 158.24
regulation 142.2
risks 158.27-39
safety 165.26-7, 30-31
  and National Identity Scheme 168.15
social networking sites 179.18
and the sexual exploitation of children 99.16, 21, 24
shopping 158.3, 30-31
  Europe 134.15-16
  and gender 134.16
social networking sites 142.35, 36, 38; 157.15; 168.34-6
  safety 179.18
suicide websites 136.37, 38, 39
surveillance 168.8, 13-14, 32-3
and terrorism 147.8-9
and travel industry 156.1, 13, 14
trends 158.1-26
see also child pornography; e-mail; safety and the Internet;
  websites
intersexuality 153.13
inter-species mixing 144.10-12
intestinal problems and eating disorders 127.5
intracytoplasmic sperm injection (ICSI) 178.8
investment in stock market 180.7
investment scams 134.27
involuntary euthanasia 152.1
involuntary smoking *see* passive smoking
iodine and vegetarian diet 140.3
iPS cells (induced pluripotent stem cells) 178.38
iridology 81.17-18
iron in the diet 88.6, 15
  red meat 140.12
  sources 140.4, 7; 176.8
  teenagers' needs 176.8
  and vegetarian diet 140.1, 3, 7
irrigation

and global water supplies 76.3, 4, 5, 19
and water shortages 76.21
Islam 148.3-4
  and anti-extremism 147.34
  and the census 148.7
  and faith schools 148.35
  festivals 148.3
  food rules 148.3-4; 11
  fundamentalist beliefs of young Muslims 147.16-17
  funerals 116.34-5
  mosque governance standards 147.34
  observance trends, Britain 148.18-19
  preventing youth extremism 148.30-31
  public perceptions of 147.26
  teaching in British Mosques 147.17-18
  and terrorism 147.15, 26-7
  see also Muslims
Islamic mortgages 181.28
Islamophobia 115.36
  and national identity 131.11
isolation, older people 159.3, 8, 17, 30
IVF *see* in vitro fertilization

J

jail *see* prison
Jedism 148.6-7
jewellery, recycling 161.24
Jews (Judaism) 148.4-5
  and the Census (2001) 148.7
  and faith schools 148.35
  food rules 148.4, 10-11
  funerals 116.33-4
  and racism laws 115.26
jihad 147.15
jobs
  distribution inequalities 149.28
  job hunting 107.31-2
  job satisfaction 107.1-2, 13; 154.18
  job security 107.1, 2
  see also employment
Jobseekers Allowance 133.33-4
joints, effects of running 162.33
journal keeping as way of remembrance 116.16
journalists
  and libel law 142.27
  protection of sources 142.22
  regulation 142.16
  talking to 142.11-14
journey length trends 119.29
  travelling to school 119.30
junk mail 134.26, 28; 161.19, 26
justice system and gender equality 154.4

K

keeping fit *see* fitness
ketamine 163.18-20
Key Stages (schools) 139.1-2, 5

Kick it Out, anti-racism campaign 118.14
kidney damage and eating disorders 127.5
Killing with Kindness campaign 130.32
killings *see* homicide; murder
kinesiology 81.2
knee repair, stem cell therapy 144.21
knife crime 177.15-16, 29-30
    sentencing 177.38-9
    statistics 177.38, 39
    young people's concerns 177.15-16
knives and the law 177.7
knowledge, globalisation of 157.1
Kyoto Protocol 151.2
    Clean Development Mechanism 151.17
    Kyoto Compliant emission reduction projects 151.21
    UK target 146.8

L

labelling
    alcohol 143.30, 31, 32
    ethical products 134.34
    GM animal feed 138.25
    GM food 138.11, 39
    products 134.1-2
labour migration 150.1-2
    see also migrant workers
lacto-ovo-vegetarians 140.2
lacto-vegetarians 140.2
lactose, and vegetarians 140.19
lads' magazines 142.29
    and body image 170.28
landfill 146.23; 1-2, 6-7, 10
    hazardous waste 161.32
    restoring sites to green space 161.33
    tax 161.12, 20, 35
landlords
    reluctant 181.17
    support services 130.29
    and tenants' rights 181.16
language
    in advertising 134.9
    barriers to employment 89.27, 35, 37
    of technology 158.16-17
    strong language on television 121.38-9
lanolin, and vegetarians 140.19
law *see* legislation
law and drugs 163.1-2, 31-9
law-making process 131.24
    citizen involvement 131.25
laxatives, effects 127.2
lead pollution 146.36
leadership in sport
    ethnic minorities 118.13
    women 118.20
learning
    effects of cannabis 128.14
    impact on homelessness 130.34-5
learning disabilities 135.33-9
    and bullying 165.2, 14-16, 17
    causes 135.33
    definition 135.33
    management of 135.34-5
    and the media 135.35
    and education 135.36-9
    see also disabled people
leaving home
    after domestic abuse 155.4-5, 6-7, 12-13, 27-8
    young people 181.26
left-wing terrorism 147.1
legal advice on arrest 177.35
legalizing drugs, potential results 163.39
legislation
    and abortion 171.1, 5-7; 11-12; 15-16
        and doctors 171.27-8
        and religion 171.18
    age discrimination 159.10, 11
    and alcohol
        drink-driving 143.24
        young people 143.2, 17
    animal experiments 169.14, 20, 23
    animal welfare 169.3, 4
    on asylum 89.3-4, 11, 12, 33, 39

Volume numbers appear first (in bold) followed by page numbers; a change in volume number is preceded by a semi-colon.

Vol. 76 The Water Crisis	**Vol. 138** A Genetically Modified Future?	**Vol. 161** Waste Issues
Vol. 78 Threatened Species	**Vol. 139** The Education Problem	**Vol. 162** Staying Fit
Vol. 81 Alternative Therapies	**Vol. 140** Vegetarian and Vegan Diets	**Vol. 163** Drugs in the UK
Vol. 88 Food and Nutrition	**Vol. 141** Mental Health	**Vol. 164** The AIDS Crisis
Vol. 89 Refugees	**Vol. 142** Media Issues	**Vol. 165** Bullying Issues
Vol. 97 Energy Matters	**Vol. 143** Problem Drinking	**Vol. 166** Marriage and Cohabitation
Vol. 99 Exploited Children	**Vol. 144** The Cloning Debate	**Vol. 167** Our Human Rights
Vol. 100 Stress and Anxiety	**Vol. 145** Smoking Trends	**Vol. 168** Privacy and Surveillance
Vol. 107 Work Issues	**Vol. 146** Sustainability and Environment	**Vol. 169** The Animal Rights Debate
Vol. 116 Grief and Loss	**Vol. 147** The Terrorism Problem	**Vol. 170** Body Image and Self-Esteem
Vol. 118 Focus on Sport	**Vol. 148** Religious Beliefs	**Vol. 171** Abortion – Rights and Ethics
Vol. 119 Transport Trends	**Vol. 149** A Classless Society?	**Vol. 172** Racial and Ethnic Discrimination
Vol. 121 The Censorship Debate	**Vol. 150** Migration and Population	**Vol. 173** Sexual Health
Vol. 124 Parenting Issues	**Vol. 151** Climate Change	**Vol. 174** Selling Sex
Vol. 125 Understanding Depression	**Vol. 152** Euthanasia and the Right to Die	**Vol. 175** Citizenship and Participation
Vol. 127 Eating Disorders	**Vol. 153** Sexual Orientation and Society	**Vol. 176** Health Issues for Young People
Vol. 128 The Cannabis Issue	**Vol. 154** The Gender Gap	**Vol. 177** Crime in the UK
Vol. 129 Gambling Trends	**Vol. 155** Domestic Abuse	**Vol. 178** Reproductive Ethics
Vol. 130 Homelessness	**Vol. 156** Travel and Tourism	**Vol. 179** Tackling Child Abuse
Vol. 133 Teen Pregnancy and Lone Parents	**Vol. 157** The Problem of Globalisation	**Vol. 180** Money and Finances
Vol. 134 Customers and Consumerism	**Vol. 158** The Internet Revolution	**Vol. 181** The Housing Issue
Vol. 135 Coping with Disability	**Vol. 159** An Ageing Population	
Vol. 136 Self-Harm	**Vol. 160** Poverty and Exclusion	

blasphemy **121**.16
and bullying
    cyberbullying **165**.25, 39
    workplace bullying **165**.33
and cannabis **128**.2, 7, 9, 26-38
on climate change **151**.17
and corporal punishment **167**.26-8
    European countries **179**.31
and domestic violence **155**.2; 28; 37-8
and drugs **163**.1-2, 33; **176**.19
on embryo research **144**.15, 17, 27-8
employment of young people **180**.20
and euthanasia **152**.1, 16-18, 29-30
    Australia **152**.19
    Belgium **152**.4, 18, 19
    Italy **152**.10-11
    Netherlands **152**.4, 18, 19
    Scotland **152**.17, 29, 30
    Switzerland **152**.18, 19
    US, Oregon state **152**.4, 18, 19, 31, 33
and film classification **121**.23-5
on food additives **88**.39
on food labelling **88**.23, 24, 25
and forced marriages **155**.17
Freedom of Information Act **142**.17-21
on gambling
    Gambling Act **129**.5, 17, 23
    and gambling at work **129**.23
    online gambling **129**.17
on gender discrimination **154**.14
and HIV transmission **164**.14
on homelessness
    England and Wales **130**.28
    Scotland **130**.5
human rights **167**.2
hunting with dogs **169**.27-9, 30-32
law-making process **131**.24
    citizen involvement **131**.25
libel and journalistic freedom **142**.27
libel and slander **142**.26
Poor Laws **149**.13
on privacy **168**.2-3
Racial and Religious Hatred Bill **121**.7, 15
and racism **115**.2, 7-8, 26
    at work **115**.11-12
on religious hatred **115**.26; **121**.7, 15
and sex **176**.21-2
Sexual Orientation Regulation **153**.35, 36, 37
and sexuality **153**.26-39
and smoking
    ban on smoking in public places **145**.11-17
    children **145**.3; **176**.13
and squatting **181**.20
and sunbeds **176**.11
on surveillance **168**.10
and tenants' rights **181**.16
and video **121**.31
video games classification **121**.32
and weapons **177**.7, 30
leisure activities
    effect of poverty **160**.2

older people **159**.3, 8
lesbians
    definition **153**.1
    having children **153**.20-22, 33-4; **178**.9-10
    and the media **142**.39
    see also gay couples; homosexuality
leukaemia, stem cell therapy **144**.21
libel **142**.26
    and journalism **142**.27
liberalisation **157**.12, 20
    see also free trade
licence fee, BBC **142**.6
licensing
    alcohol sales **143**.2
    gambling **129**.5, 8, 23
    hybrid embryo research **144**.14
    stem cell research **144**.17, 27-8
licensing hours and crime **143**.23
life chances
    and teenage parenthood **133**.10
life expectancy **150**.32, 35; **159**.6
    and alcohol consumption **143**.13
    and obesity **176**.7
    HIV patients **164**.8-9
    and poverty **160**.38
    and smoking **145**.21
    and social class **149**.15
    ways of increasing **159**.32-4
    UK **159**.3, 34
life insurance cover and home buying **181**.24
life stages and social identity **149**.23
lifestyle
    and ageing **159**.2, 34
    and life expectancy **159**.33-4
    sports **118**.1
    stress and changes in **100**.19
    and weight loss **162**.20
lifetime debt **180**.11-12
light bulbs, recycling **161**.24
light therapy for Seasonal Affective Disorder **125**.18, 37; **141**.35
limited human rights **167**.4
listening **141**.35-6
    as help for bereaved **116**.14-15
listeria **88**.28-9
literacy
    employees' literacy problems **139**.17
    and poverty **160**.28
litter **161**.15-16, 21
live animal transport **169**.10
liver damage and stem cell therapy **144**.22
living standards and water consumption **76**.8
living wills *see* advance directives (living wills)
LL601 rice **138**.31-4
loans **180**.27
    student **139**.34; **180**.28, 33
    see also credit; debt
local authorities
    duty to house **130**.2-3
    and greenfield development **181**.22
    homelessness prevention funds **130**.29-30
    homelessness strategies **130**.28

and housing young people 181.26-7
and self-build projects 181.30
and social housing 181.29
and surveillance 168.20-21
and tourism 156.9
see also council tenants
Local Authority care leavers, and homelessness 130.11, 14
local communities, effects of tourism 156.22
lodgers' rights 181.16
logging, destructive 146.30
London
   bombings
      and faith hate crime 115.27
      impact on Muslims 115.36
   congestion charging 119.12, 38
   counter-terrorism measures 147.31
   illegal radio stations 142.7
   and migrant workers 150.11
   multicultural tolerance 115.23
   Olympics and tourism 156.13
lone parents 124.33-5; 133.28-38
   benefits available 133.33-6
   benefits claimed 133.32, 36
   children of 124.22, 33-4; 133.28, 31
   and divorce 124.33-4
   and employment 133.28
   help for 133.37-8
   and household income 133.28, 30
   and housing advice 133.37
   statistics 124.35; 133.28-32; 166.4, 15
   teenage 133.28
   see also teenage pregnancies
loneliness
   after bereavement 116.4, 19
   after divorce 166.23
   older people 159.3, 8, 17, 30
long-term illness 159.4
lotteries 129.2
   scams 134.26
   see also National Lottery
low carbon technologies 97.4
low-cost home ownership 181.25

low impact policing and football hooliganism 118.8
low income families
   subsidised broadband access 158.18
low income workers 160.5
low self-esteem (LSE) 170.2, 3
   and bullying 165.16
   causes of 170.8
   and eating disorders 127.2
   and self-harm 136.2
loyalty cards and personal data 168.8
LPG vehicles 119.20
LSD 163.6
lung cancer 145.34
   and cannabis use 128.17, 19, 28

M

magazines
   influence on body image 170.28
   and sex education 142.28, 29
magic mushrooms 163.6
magnetic field therapy 81.30, 31
maintained schools, definition 135.36
maintenance payments 133.37
malaria 76.6
   Millennium Development Goals 160.32
male stereotyping as barrier to university entrance 139.38
male violence, attitudes to 177.5
malignant melanoma 176.10-11
malnutrition 176.4
   see also hunger
managers
   gender gap 154.17
   gender pay gap 154.38
   and workplace stress 100.18, 25
mandatory eviction 181.16
manic depression *see* bipolar affective disorder
manufacturing sector employment 107.7, 10
marijuana *see* herbal cannabis
marine ecosystems, effect of climate change 151.9
marital status and health 166.15

Volume numbers appear first (in bold) followed by page numbers; a change in volume number is preceded by a semi-colon.

Vol. 76 The Water Crisis
Vol. 78 Threatened Species
Vol. 81 Alternative Therapies
Vol. 88 Food and Nutrition
Vol. 89 Refugees
Vol. 97 Energy Matters
Vol. 99 Exploited Children
Vol. 100 Stress and Anxiety
Vol. 107 Work Issues
Vol. 116 Grief and Loss
Vol. 118 Focus on Sport
Vol. 119 Transport Trends
Vol. 121 The Censorship Debate
Vol. 124 Parenting Issues
Vol. 125 Understanding Depression
Vol. 127 Eating Disorders
Vol. 128 The Cannabis Issue
Vol. 129 Gambling Trends
Vol. 130 Homelessness
Vol. 133 Teen Pregnancy and Lone Parents
Vol. 134 Customers and Consumerism
Vol. 135 Coping with Disability
Vol. 136 Self-Harm

Vol. 138 A Genetically Modified Future?
Vol. 139 The Education Problem
Vol. 140 Vegetarian and Vegan Diets
Vol. 141 Mental Health
Vol. 142 Media Issues
Vol. 143 Problem Drinking
Vol. 144 The Cloning Debate
Vol. 145 Smoking Trends
Vol. 146 Sustainability and Environment
Vol. 147 The Terrorism Problem
Vol. 148 Religious Beliefs
Vol. 149 A Classless Society?
Vol. 150 Migration and Population
Vol. 151 Climate Change
Vol. 152 Euthanasia and the Right to Die
Vol. 153 Sexual Orientation and Society
Vol. 154 The Gender Gap
Vol. 155 Domestic Abuse
Vol. 156 Travel and Tourism
Vol. 157 The Problem of Globalisation
Vol. 158 The Internet Revolution
Vol. 159 An Ageing Population
Vol. 160 Poverty and Exclusion

Vol. 161 Waste Issues
Vol. 162 Staying Fit
Vol. 163 Drugs in the UK
Vol. 164 The AIDS Crisis
Vol. 165 Bullying Issues
Vol. 166 Marriage and Cohabitation
Vol. 167 Our Human Rights
Vol. 168 Privacy and Surveillance
Vol. 169 The Animal Rights Debate
Vol. 170 Body Image and Self-Esteem
Vol. 171 Abortion – Rights and Ethics
Vol. 172 Racial and Ethnic Discrimination
Vol. 173 Sexual Health
Vol. 174 Selling Sex
Vol. 175 Citizenship and Participation
Vol. 176 Health Issues for Young People
Vol. 177 Crime in the UK
Vol. 178 Reproductive Ethics
Vol. 179 Tackling Child Abuse
Vol. 180 Money and Finances
Vol. 181 The Housing Issue

marker-assisted selection (MAS) 138.37-9
marker genes 138.4
market size, gambling industry 129.4
    National Lottery 129.9, 10
    online gambling 129.17, 19
marketing alcohol to young people 143.17
marriage 166.1-20
    age at 166.4, 6
    arranged marriages 166.16
    attitudes to 166.1-2, 7, 9-11
    births outside 124.22
    and Civil Partnerships 153.26
    'common law' marriage 166.12
    expectations of cohabiting partners 166.2, 7
    forced marriages 155.16-18; 166.17-20
    and HIV/AIDS 96.24-5, 29, 34, 35
    institutional elements 166.2-3
    inter-ethnic 115.25
    male and female attitudes to 166.3
    reasons for marrying 166.2
    reasons for not marrying 166.2, 9-11
    relational elements 166.2-3
    statistics 166.4, 6
    and stepfamilies see stepfamilies
    unhappy 166.7-8
mass surveillance 168.6
massage 81.4
    see also aromatherapy
maternal health, Millennium Development Goals 160.31-2
maternal mortality 154.12
maternity leave 107.16, 21
mathematics, A-level performance 139.18
mature students 139.30, 32
maximum working hours 107.30-1
means tested benefits 160.23, 24
meat consumption 88.6, 26, 31; 140.12-13, 15-18
    alternatives to meat 140.19, 26
    effects 140.13
    and fat 140.12
    game as food source 140.15, 17
    health issues 140.13, 21, 30
    illegal meat 88.39
    nutrients 140.12, 14
meat production
    and animal welfare 169.10
    effects of 140.13, 16-17
    free range 169.11-12
    intensively farmed chickens 169.13
    organic 140.29-30
media
    accountability 142.17-30
    and body image 127.23; 170.22, 23, 24, 28, 30-31, 38
        and eating disorders 127.25-6, 27
    breaking ethnic stereotypes 115.22
    control 142.1-16
    convergence 142.1-2
    and football-related violence 118.7
    government control 121.1
    government use of 121.17-18
    and homosexuality 153.23-5
    impact 142.31-9

intrusion 142.23, 25, 26
mergers 142.4
over-reaction to terrorism 147.10-11
ownership 121.4-5
and people with learning difficulties 135.35
portrayal of disabled people 135.29, 32
and pressure on athletes to use drugs 118.29
and privacy 168.7, 28-9
and public perception of crime 177.3-4
and suicide 136.37-9
teenage magazines 142.28
violence see violence, media
women in the media 154.11
and women's sport 118.21-2
see also films; Internet; newspapers; radio; television
mediation
    and divorce 166.26, 35, 38-9
    and homelessness prevention 130.30
medical abortion ('the abortion pill') 171.2, 35, 36
medical benefits, GM crops 138.9-10
    see also pharming
medical profession
    attitudes to abortion 171.25-8, 34
    attitudes to euthanasia 152.7, 8, 24-6, 27-8
    effects of legalizing euthanasia 152.7
    see also doctors
medical research and animal experimentation 140.32-3;
    144.34
medical tourism 156.4-5
medical treatment
    and the Mental Capacity Act 152.37, 38
    for obesity 162.2-3, 6
    patient's right to refuse 152.2, 10-11
    premature babies 152.4, 32, 34
    withdrawing or withholding 152.3, 5-6
    see also palliative care
medical waste disposal 161.24
medically-assisted dying see physician-assisted suicide
medicinal drug use 163.1
    cannabis 128.4, 28, 36, 37
        and the law 128.37
        multiple sclerosis 128.36, 37
medicines
    and alcohol 143.10
    and banned substances in sport 118.32-3
    effects on fertility 178.4, 5
    from GM crops (pharming) 138.4, 9-10, 20-22
melanoma 176.10-11
memories of the deceased see remembrance of the deceased
memory, effect of cannabis use 128.4-5
men
    and alcohol
        alcohol consumption 143.8, 31
        safe limits 143.26, 34
    attitudes 154.16
    body image and lads' magazines 170.28
    and compulsive shopping 134.14
    and depression 125.13-15
    and domestic violence 155.12-13
    and eating disorders 127.3
    fertility problems 178.3, 4-5, 8

fertility and smoking 145.32
gender stereotypes 154.7-8
homosexual activity 133.2
and household financial roles 180.18-19
marriage expectations 166.3
and mental ill-health 141.1
and online shopping 134.16
and self-harm 136.2
and sexual health 96.13
and smoking 145.21, 22
and stress 100.13, 19
and suicide 136.33, 35, 36
see also boys and young men; fathers; gay men
mental health 141.2, 34-6; 176.4, 29-39
and abortion 171.9-10, 33
assessment after attempted suicide 136.28
awareness of 176.31-2
benefits of exercise 141.34, 39; 162.37, 38
and cannabis 128.5, 8, 14-15; 163.35
children 141.37; 176.29-30; 36-7
and diet 125.11-12; 141.30-31, 34
and disability 135.4
and domestic violence 155.5
education in 141.37
and homeless people 130.11, 20, 27
and older people 159.4
 see also dementia
risk factors 176.29
and smoking 145.38-9
statistics 125.16
and terrorism threat 147.12
treatment 176.30
and workplace stress 100.17-18, 20
young people 176.4, 29-39
see also dementia; depression
mental illness
attitudes to 141.25, 27
and cannabis 163.35
children 141.1, 20-21
and criminal behaviour 141.2, 22
definition 141.1
and eating disorders 127.9-10

genetic predisposition to 141.24
help for people with 141.34-6
and homelessness 130.11, 20, 27
and homosexuality 153.3, 6
and poverty 141.2, 22
prevalence 141.1
see also depression; schizophrenia
mentalities 149.6
mercy killing (non-voluntary euthanasia) 152.1, 3
metabolism 88.15
effect of smoking 145.26, 30-31
metals recycling 161.24
aluminium 161.22, 27
methamphetamine (crystal meth) 163.16-17, 32
methane
emissions from agriculture 151.7
trapping 151.36
methyl alcohol (meths) 143.1-2
microbes 88.27, 28-9
microbicides 96.34, 35
microgeneration of energy 151.39
middle-classes 149.19-20
residential mobility 149.26
and university application discrimination 149.7
mifepristone (the abortion pill) 171.2
migrant workers
exploitation 150.14, 15, 19, 20, 22
need for 150.11
and slavery 167.21
UK 150.4-5
migrants
attitudes to 150.3, 13-14, 17, 18-19
and crime 150.12, 13
definition 150.21
and economic growth 150.11, 17
and sexual health 150.21-3
see also migrant workers
migration 150.1-27, 35
data collection 150.5
definition 150.4, 21
effect on environment 150.26-7
global trends 150.1-2

Volume numbers appear first (in bold) followed by page numbers; a change in volume number is preceded by a semi-colon.

Vol. 76 The Water Crisis
Vol. 78 Threatened Species
Vol. 81 Alternative Therapies
Vol. 88 Food and Nutrition
Vol. 89 Refugees
Vol. 97 Energy Matters
Vol. 99 Exploited Children
Vol. 100 Stress and Anxiety
Vol. 107 Work Issues
Vol. 116 Grief and Loss
Vol. 118 Focus on Sport
Vol. 119 Transport Trends
Vol. 121 The Censorship Debate
Vol. 124 Parenting Issues
Vol. 125 Understanding Depression
Vol. 127 Eating Disorders
Vol. 128 The Cannabis Issue
Vol. 129 Gambling Trends
Vol. 130 Homelessness
Vol. 133 Teen Pregnancy and Lone Parents
Vol. 134 Customers and Consumerism
Vol. 135 Coping with Disability
Vol. 136 Self-Harm
Vol. 138 A Genetically Modified Future?
Vol. 139 The Education Problem
Vol. 140 Vegetarian and Vegan Diets
Vol. 141 Mental Health
Vol. 142 Media Issues
Vol. 143 Problem Drinking
Vol. 144 The Cloning Debate
Vol. 145 Smoking Trends
Vol. 146 Sustainability and Environment
Vol. 147 The Terrorism Problem
Vol. 148 Religious Beliefs
Vol. 149 A Classless Society?
Vol. 150 Migration and Population
Vol. 151 Climate Change
Vol. 152 Euthanasia and the Right to Die
Vol. 153 Sexual Orientation and Society
Vol. 154 The Gender Gap
Vol. 155 Domestic Abuse
Vol. 156 Travel and Tourism
Vol. 157 The Problem of Globalisation
Vol. 158 The Internet Revolution
Vol. 159 An Ageing Population
Vol. 160 Poverty and Exclusion
Vol. 161 Waste Issues
Vol. 162 Staying Fit
Vol. 163 Drugs in the UK
Vol. 164 The AIDS Crisis
Vol. 165 Bullying Issues
Vol. 166 Marriage and Cohabitation
Vol. 167 Our Human Rights
Vol. 168 Privacy and Surveillance
Vol. 169 The Animal Rights Debate
Vol. 170 Body Image and Self-Esteem
Vol. 171 Abortion – Rights and Ethics
Vol. 172 Racial and Ethnic Discrimination
Vol. 173 Sexual Health
Vol. 174 Selling Sex
Vol. 175 Citizenship and Participation
Vol. 176 Health Issues for Young People
Vol. 177 Crime in the UK
Vol. 178 Reproductive Ethics
Vol. 179 Tackling Child Abuse
Vol. 180 Money and Finances
Vol. 181 The Housing Issue

lack of accurate data **150**.6, 19, 23
    reasons for **150**.21, 24-5
    statistics **150**.4, 8-9, 23, 26, 35
    and unemployment **150**.9-10
    see also asylum seekers; immigration
military globalisation **157**.2
milk
    from cloned cows **144**.36-8, 39
    vegetarian alternatives **140**.22, 26
Millennium Development Goals **160**.26, 28, 20-32
    and gender discrimination **154**.14
    and sustainable development **146**.1-2
minerals and vegetarian diets **140**.3
minicabs and disabled people **135**.9
minimum income standard **160**.8; **180**.6
minimum wage **107**.31
ministers of religion **148**.1
minority ethnic groups *see* ethnic minorities
miscegenation *see* mixed-race relationships
mitochondrial DNA **144**.17
mixed-faith relationships **115**.39
mixed-race families **124**.36-7
mixed-race people, Britain **115**.24-5
    as victims of crime **115**.10
mixed-race relationships **115**.22-3, 24-5
MNCs *see* (multi-national corporations)
mobile phones
    bullying by **165**.23
    concerns about **158**.12, 32
    and gambling **129**.18, 26
    household ownership **134**.5
    information logging **168**.8
    and social networking **158**.11-12
    usage trends **158**.4-5; 11-14
mock elections for young people **131**.27
models of disability **135**.1
Mohammed, Danish cartoons of **121**.10-13, 15-16; **142**.34
money
    attitudes to, and social class **149**.19-20
    financial abuse **159**.16
    money management **180**.7-19
    students **180**.28-9, 32-3
    worries
        non-traditional families **124**.20
    see also banks; credit; debt; incomes; wages
mood stabilising drugs **125**.19, 25
moral decisions and humanism **148**.14-16
moral decline, Britain **148**.17
moral rights
    of animals **169**.1
    of embryos **178**.33-4
morphine **152**.26-7
mortality rates **150**.32
mortgages **181**.24, 28
    help for lone parents **133**.34
    lifetime mortgages **180**.23
    mortgage lending **134**.25
mosques
    improving governance standards **147**.34
    teaching in British mosques **147**.17-18
mothers

    and abortion rights **171**.28
    abortion to save mother's life **171**.17, 22
    effect on children's body image **170**.24
    employment patterns **107**.26; **149**.28; **154**.29
    full-time **124**.12
    HIV transmission to children **164**.3, 25, 27, 29-30, 31, 38
    identity confusion **149**.4-5
    and poverty **160**.15
    share of household tasks **124**.11
    see also working mothers
motor neurone disease (MND) and stem cell research **144**.32-3
motoring
    costs **119**.14
    and disability **135**.7
    spending on **134**.4, 25
    trends **119**.7-9
    see also cars
motorways, active traffic management **119**.37
mourning *see* grief
MPs and General Elections **131**.18
multiculturalism
    Britain **156**.11
    British Muslims support for **115**.34
    as hindrance to British identity **131**.10
    London **115**.23
multi-faith schools **148**.32-3
multi-infarct dementia (vascular dementia) **141**.6
multinational corporations (MNCs) **157**.6, 11
    and anti-globalisation campaigners **157**.30-31
    employment **157**.13
multinational water corporations, and the privatisation of water supplies **76**.22, 23, 29-30
multiple births and IVF **178**.6-7
    health problems **178**.21-2
multiple embryo transfers **178**.8
multiple identity concept of national identity **131**.10
multiple personality disorder **141**.12
multiple sclerosis (MS)
    and complementary medicine **81**.30-1
    and depression **125**.5
    and the medicinal use of cannabis **128**.36, 37
multiracial families **124**.36-7
multiracialism, Britain **115**.3, 23, 24-5, 38
multisensory alarms in cars **119**.19
murder, bereavement by **116**.8
muscle dysmorphia **127**.19
music and mental health **141**.36
Muslims
    British, feelings of identity **131**.9
    fears after London bombings **115**.36
    support for integration **115**.34
    young Muslims and fundamentalism **147**.16-17
    see also Islam

N

nalbuphine hydrochloride **118**.35
nalmefene **129**.39
name changing and civil partnerships **153**.28

names for racial identity **115**.4-5

nappies, waste disposal **161**.1 5, 29

National Curriculum **139**.1-2, 5-6
    and alcohol education **143**.20
    pupils opinions **139**.7
    and specialist diplomas **139**.25

National DNA Database **168**.7, 11-12

National Health Service **149**.13-14
    anti-bullying strategies **165**.36
    and older people **159**.4

national identity **131**.1-14
    cards *see* identity cards
    effect of devolution **131**.6
    and ethnic groups **131**.8
    non-white ethnic groups **115**.38

National Identity Scheme **168**.14-19

National Lottery **129**.9-13
    good causes **129**.9
    Olympic Games funding **129**.9
    online, and under 16s **129**.12-13
    and social mobility **149**.22
    and under 16s **129**.11-13

natural burial **134**.31

natural cloning **144**.1

natural gas vehicles **119**.20-21

natural medicine *see* complementary medicine (CM)

natural resources **146**.9

naturopathy **81**.2, 19

negative body image *see* body image, negative

negative resource transfers **157**.7

negative thinking **170**.6

neglect
    children **179**.3
        reporting **179**.7
        signs **179**.5
        taking children into care **179**.10-11
    and older people **159**.17

nervous system diseases and depression **125**.5

neurobiology and gambling **129**.6

neurosis **141**.1

neurotransmitters **141**.9

news
    attitudes to **142**.31-3
    being interviewed **142**.11-12
    effect of media ownership **142**.5
    sources **142**.33
    women in news media **154**.11

news manipulation **121**.6

newspapers **142**.8-9
    advertising **134**.8
    cartoons of Mohammed **121**.10-13, 15-16; **142**.34
    and Freedom of Information Act **142**.17
    mergers **142**.4
    ownership **121**.4-5
    readership **142**.8
    sales **142**.9
    as source of news **142**.33

NHS (National Health Service)
    and complementary medicine **81**.4, 21
        costs of **81**.31
        effectiveness of **81**.22
        funding **81**.27, 29, 36
        and multiple sclerosis **81**.30-1
        osteopathy **81**.7
        reflexology **81**.17, 31
        support for **81**.30-1
    and eating disorders **127**.28
    and HIV treatments **96**.21, 22

nicotine
    addiction **145**.25-7, 35
    chemical content **145**.25
    children **145**.2-3
    effects on the body **145**.25-6
    gum **145**.37
    inhalator **145**.37
    nasal spray **145**.37
    patches **145**.37
    and young people **145**.20
    replacement therapy **145**.33, 37
    toxicity **145**.27
    withdrawal symptoms **145**.26-7

nitrogen oxide (NOx) emissions **146**.35
    agriculture **151**.7
    transport **119**.15, 16

Volume numbers appear first (in bold) followed by page numbers; a change in volume number is preceded by a semi-colon.

Vol. 76 The Water Crisis
Vol. 78 Threatened Species
Vol. 81 Alternative Therapies
Vol. 88 Food and Nutrition
Vol. 89 Refugees
Vol. 97 Energy Matters
Vol. 99 Exploited Children
Vol. 100 Stress and Anxiety
Vol. 107 Work Issues
Vol. 116 Grief and Loss
Vol. 118 Focus on Sport
Vol. 119 Transport Trends
Vol. 121 The Censorship Debate
Vol. 124 Parenting Issues
Vol. 125 Understanding Depression
Vol. 127 Eating Disorders
Vol. 128 The Cannabis Issue
Vol. 129 Gambling Trends
Vol. 130 Homelessness
Vol. 133 Teen Pregnancy and Lone Parents
Vol. 134 Customers and Consumerism
Vol. 135 Coping with Disability
Vol. 136 Self-Harm

Vol. 138 A Genetically Modified Future?
Vol. 139 The Education Problem
Vol. 140 Vegetarian and Vegan Diets
Vol. 141 Mental Health
Vol. 142 Media Issues
Vol. 143 Problem Drinking
Vol. 144 The Cloning Debate
Vol. 145 Smoking Trends
Vol. 146 Sustainability and Environment
Vol. 147 The Terrorism Problem
Vol. 148 Religious Beliefs
Vol. 149 A Classless Society?
Vol. 150 Migration and Population
Vol. 151 Climate Change
Vol. 152 Euthanasia and the Right to Die
Vol. 153 Sexual Orientation and Society
Vol. 154 The Gender Gap
Vol. 155 Domestic Abuse
Vol. 156 Travel and Tourism
Vol. 157 The Problem of Globalisation
Vol. 158 The Internet Revolution
Vol. 159 An Ageing Population
Vol. 160 Poverty and Exclusion

Vol. 161 Waste Issues
Vol. 162 Staying Fit
Vol. 163 Drugs in the UK
Vol. 164 The AIDS Crisis
Vol. 165 Bullying Issues
Vol. 166 Marriage and Cohabitation
Vol. 167 Our Human Rights
Vol. 168 Privacy and Surveillance
Vol. 169 The Animal Rights Debate
Vol. 170 Body Image and Self-Esteem
Vol. 171 Abortion – Rights and Ethics
Vol. 172 Racial and Ethnic Discrimination
Vol. 173 Sexual Health
Vol. 174 Selling Sex
Vol. 175 Citizenship and Participation
Vol. 176 Health Issues for Young People
Vol. 177 Crime in the UK
Vol. 178 Reproductive Ethics
Vol. 179 Tackling Child Abuse
Vol. 180 Money and Finances
Vol. 181 The Housing Issue

no-earner families **149**.28
non-contributory benefits **160**.23
non-governmental organisations (NGOs) **157**.7
    and global water supplies **76**.30, 31
non-maintained special schools **135**.36
non-means tested benefits **160**.23
non-reproductive cloning *see* therapeutic cloning
non-traditional families **124**.20-21
non-traditional jobs for women **154**.31-2
non-violent direct action **121**.14
non-voluntary euthanasia **152**.1, 3
nuclear power **97**.3-4, 19-23; **151**.29
    building new power stations **97**.21-2
    and clean-up of nuclear weapons material **97**.23
    and climate change **97**.19-20, 21, 22
    costs of **97**.6
    debate over **97**.7
    disadvantages of **97**.2, 7, 8
    and electricity generation **97**.3-4, 22-3
    environmental issues surrounding **97**.2, 4
    and nuclear waste **97**.20, 22, 23
    and radioactive discharges **97**.20
    and renewable energy **97**.6, 7, 19, 21
    and terrorism **97**.20
number plate recognition **168**.9
numbness and traumatic bereavement **116**.10
    see also shock
numeracy problems, employees **139**.17
nurses, migration from developing countries **150**.15
nutrition
    and ageing **159**.2
    and meat **140**.12, 14
    and mental health **141**.30-31, 34
    and need for intensive farming **169**.12
    teenagers **176**.8-9
    vegetarians **140**.3-4, 6, 11
    see also diet; healthy eating
nutritional supplements **118**.28
    and anti-doping rules **118**.33
NVQs (National Vocational Qualifications) **139**.4

O

obesity **88**.4, 9-11; **127**.32-9; **162**.1-10
    avoidance *see* weight management
    and Body Mass Index (BMI) **162**.1, 4, 5, 23
    and bullying **165**.8-9
    causes **162**.2, 5, 8
    in children *see* childhood obesity
    definitions **127**.33; **162**.1, 4
    discrimination **162**.21
    economic costs **88**.4; **127**.33-4, 37
    and genetics **127**.35
    government strategies **162**.4-5, 9-10, 17-18, 22-3
    and health **127**.32, 34; **162**.1-2, 5, 6, 7, 19, 25; **176**.7
    and life expectancy **176**.7
    measurement **162**.1
        children **127**.36, 37
    predictions **162**.10, 18, 19
    statistics **127**.32, 33, 34; **162**.1, 5, 6, 7, 18

    treatment **162**.2-3, 6, 20
    in the workplace **162**.21
    worldwide **162**.7
        see also weight management
    and young people **176**.2, 3, 7, 9
    see also body weight
obestatin (appetite-suppressing hormone) **127**.38-9
obsessions **141**.17
obsessive compulsive disorder (OCD) **141**.17
ocean plants and CO_2 removal **151**.25
occupational choice, women **154**.30
    non-traditional **154**.31-2
occupational social class **149**.21
Ofcom **121**.36
    and illegal broadcasting **142**.7
    and media mergers **142**.4
offending and mental health problems **125**.16
offensive language, television **121**.38-9
official debt **157**.7
offsetting carbon **151**.20-22, 33-5
offshore wind farms **97**.12, 16, 26
offshoring **157**.35-6
oil
    depletion of resources **97**.8, 10
    leakages **97**.3
    recycling **161**.5, 23, 28
    and renewable energy **97**.10
older people
    abuse of **159**.4, 6, 16-18
    as carers **159**.4, 5
    and depression **125**.22-3
    excessive drinking **143**.9-10, 30
    and health **159**.4, 6, 8, 35-9
    and homelessness **130**.17-18
    in employment **159**.10, 15
    media consumption **158**.4
    and mental health problems **125**.16; **141**.2
    and self-harm **136**.20
    spending **159**.19
    worldwide **159**.5, 6
    UK **159**.3-4, 7-8
older women and IVF **178**.17, 19-20
older workers **107**.12-13; **159**.10, 15
    and age discrimination **159**.4, 8-13
Olympic Games
    and China's human rights **167**.23-4
    drug testing **118**.25
    National Lottery funding **129**.9
omega 3 fatty acids
    and attention-deficit hyperactivity disorder **141**.19
    in eggs **140**.39
    in meat **140**.12, 21
one-parent families *see* lone parents
one planet economy **146**.8
online brands **142**.35
online bullying *see* cyberbullying
online child sexual abuse **179**.15-16, 17
online crime **158**.3, 33-4, 35, 36
online dating scams **134**.27
online divorces **166**.27

online entertainments 158.21-2

online fraud 134.26-9

online gambling 129.17-18, 19-25
   and addiction 129.21-2
   Europe 129.20
   National Lottery games and under 16s 129.12-13
   participation rates 129.17, 19
   poker, underage 129.25
   at work 129.22-4

online gaming addiction 158.39

online journalism register 142.16

online learning 139.28

online retail see Internet shopping

online safety, social networking 179.18

online surveillance 168.13-14, 32-3

online terrorism 147.8-9

online travel booking 156.1, 13, 14; 158.3

onlineaholism 142.37

opiates/opioids 163.5, 25

opium production 163.25

Oregon State, euthanasia 152.4, 18, 19, 31, 33

organ donation 116.31
   and HIV transmission 164.1

organ transplants see therapeutic cloning

organic farming 146.25, 27
   animal welfare 140.35-6
   meat production 140.29-30
   unable to meet demand for food 140.36-7

organic food 88.13-14, 18, 33, 34
   and Fairtrade 134.37

organic shops 134.30, 31

organic waste, composting 161.19, 28-9, 30

orthorexia nervosa 127.19

orphans, AIDS 96.39; 164.6-7

osteopathy 81.6-7, 23, 36

osteoporosis and chiropractic 81.9

out-of-school learning 139.27-8

outdoor activities
   and interfaith relations 148.31

outdoor (released) GMOs 138.12

outreach teams for homeless people 130.31

overdoses see drug overdoses

overdrafts 134.22, 24; 180.26-7

overseas students 139.30, 31, 32

overseas travel trends 119.1; 156.1-2, 4-5

overseas visitors to UK 156.3-4, 10, 13

overseas workers, UK dependence on 146.6

overweight people 127.32, 33
   children 119.31
   see also obesity

overworking 154.18

ovulation disorders 178.4

ownership of the media 121.4-5
   effect on news 142.5
   mergers 142.4
   newspapers 142.9

ozone and air pollution 146.35

ozone layer depletion 151.4

P

packaging waste 161.4, 5, 12

paedophiles
   disclosure of 179.20-21
   help for 179.22-3
   see also child pornography; sex offenders

pain
   absence during self-harm 136.1
   definition 152.2
   rights of animals to avoid pain 169.1
   suffered by experimental animals 169.14-16

pain relief
   and acupuncture 81.5
   see also palliative care

painkillers, misuse 163.14-15

paint, disposal of 161.23

Pakistani pupils and education 115.18

Palestinian terrorist groups 147.4

palliative care 152.1-2, 5, 9, 22, 27
   effect of legalizing euthanasia 152.4
   limits of 152.10

pancreas repair, stem cell therapy 144.21

panic attacks after bereavement 116.4

Volume numbers appear first (in bold) followed by page numbers; a change in volume number is preceded by a semi-colon.

Vol. 76 The Water Crisis
Vol. 78 Threatened Species
Vol. 81 Alternative Therapies
Vol. 88 Food and Nutrition
Vol. 89 Refugees
Vol. 97 Energy Matters
Vol. 99 Exploited Children
Vol. 100 Stress and Anxiety
Vol. 107 Work Issues
Vol. 116 Grief and Loss
Vol. 118 Focus on Sport
Vol. 119 Transport Trends
Vol. 121 The Censorship Debate
Vol. 124 Parenting Issues
Vol. 125 Understanding Depression
Vol. 127 Eating Disorders
Vol. 128 The Cannabis Issue
Vol. 129 Gambling Trends
Vol. 130 Homelessness
Vol. 133 Teen Pregnancy and Lone Parents
Vol. 134 Customers and Consumerism
Vol. 135 Coping with Disability
Vol. 136 Self-Harm

Vol. 138 A Genetically Modified Future?
Vol. 139 The Education Problem
Vol. 140 Vegetarian and Vegan Diets
Vol. 141 Mental Health
Vol. 142 Media Issues
Vol. 143 Problem Drinking
Vol. 144 The Cloning Debate
Vol. 145 Smoking Trends
Vol. 146 Sustainability and Environment
Vol. 147 The Terrorism Problem
Vol. 148 Religious Beliefs
Vol. 149 A Classless Society?
Vol. 150 Migration and Population
Vol. 151 Climate Change
Vol. 152 Euthanasia and the Right to Die
Vol. 153 Sexual Orientation and Society
Vol. 154 The Gender Gap
Vol. 155 Domestic Abuse
Vol. 156 Travel and Tourism
Vol. 157 The Problem of Globalisation
Vol. 158 The Internet Revolution
Vol. 159 An Ageing Population
Vol. 160 Poverty and Exclusion

Vol. 161 Waste Issues
Vol. 162 Staying Fit
Vol. 163 Drugs in the UK
Vol. 164 The AIDS Crisis
Vol. 165 Bullying Issues
Vol. 166 Marriage and Cohabitation
Vol. 167 Our Human Rights
Vol. 168 Privacy and Surveillance
Vol. 169 The Animal Rights Debate
Vol. 170 Body Image and Self-Esteem
Vol. 171 Abortion – Rights and Ethics
Vol. 172 Racial and Ethnic Discrimination
Vol. 173 Sexual Health
Vol. 174 Selling Sex
Vol. 175 Citizenship and Participation
Vol. 176 Health Issues for Young People
Vol. 177 Crime in the UK
Vol. 178 Reproductive Ethics
Vol. 179 Tackling Child Abuse
Vol. 180 Money and Finances
Vol. 181 The Housing Issue

paper **161.**5, 22
  recycling **161.**24, 26
Paralympic Games, National Lottery funding **129.**9
paranoia **141.**5
parasuicide **136.**24
parental child abduction **166.**36
Parental Guidance (PG) classification **121.**29
parental leave **107.**21
  for adoption **178.**16
parental relationships, effect on children **166.**4-5, 29-32
parental responsibility **124.**4; **133.**39; **153.**33; **166.**26-7, 34
  cohabiting parents **166.**14-15
parental rights **153.**33-4
parenting **124.**1-19
  styles **124.**8
parenting orders **177.**18
parents
  absence due to divorce, effect on children **124.**34
  and adult children **124.**3, 14-15
  and alcohol
    alcohol abuse **143.**37
    influence on young people **143.**5, 17
  authoritarian **124.**8
  authoritative **124.**8
  celebrity role models **124.**6
  and child labour **99.**3
  and children as consumers **134.**12
  and children's body image **170.**24
  and children's mental health **176.**29-30
  and children's television viewing **121.**26, 27, 32
  and children's video game use **121.**32-3
  cohabiting **166.**14-15
  and corporal punishment **179.**30, 33, 35
  death of **116.**12-13
  discussing eating disorders **127.**25
  education as factor in university application **149.**7, 31
  fathers' rights and responsibilities
  fears over child safety **124.**13-14
  feelings of failure **124.**16-17
  homosexual **153.**20-22
  of lesbians and gay people **153.**9-10
  with mental health problems **141.**24-5
  non-traditional families **124.**20-21
  parenting skills **124.**2
  parenting styles **124.**8
  permissive **124.**8
  removing children from **179.**10-11
  responsibilities **124.**4, 5; **133.**39
  rights **133.**39
  rights to information on sex offenders **179.**20-21
  and self-harm by children **136.**14
  sex education involvement **133.**12, 15
  and smacking **179.**33
  smoking, effects on children **145.**2, 32-3
  and stress **100.**13
  and student finance **139.**34, 35
  support for **124.**5, 6, 16-17
  support for first-time buyers **181.**1
  supporting adult children **124.**3
  of teenagers **124.**16-17
  unmarried **124.**22

  see also birth parents; divorce; families; fathers; lone parents; mothers; working parents
parking
  concessions for disabled people **135.**7-8
  illegal **119.**9
Parkinson's disease
  and dementia **141.**6
  and depression **125.**5
Parliament **131.**15
  parliamentary authority and Human Rights Act **167.**5
  women in **154.**4, 6, 12
part-time jobs **107.**17, 18, 19, 22
  and the pay gap **154.**6, 36
  and students **139.**35
partial (host) surrogacy **178.**7, 13
participation in sport **118.**9
  adults **118.**1
  female **118.**18-20
  school team sports **118.**4
  young people **118.**2
particulates emissions **119.**15
parties, political *see* political parties
passive euthanasia **152.**5
passive smoking **145.**2, 28-9
  effect on children **145.**2, 28-9
passports **89.**33
patents **138.**4
  genes **138.**23
paternity leave **107.**21
pathological gambling *see* compulsive gambling
patient confidentiality *see* confidentiality
patients' rights
  and doctors' rights, abortion **171.**28
  to refuse treatment **152.**2, 10-11
pay gap *see* gender pay gap
PE in schools **118.**3
peaceful protesting **121.**14
pedestrians and road accidents **119.**5, 30-31
peer education programmes, HIV/AIDS **164.**18
peer mentoring, anti-bullying **165.**18
peer pressure
  on athletes to use drugs **118.**29
  and drinking behaviour **143.**17
  and drug use **128.**10
  and smoking **145.**4
peer support
  and bullying **165.**18
  and self-harm **136.**8, 16, 18
peer-to-peer (P2P) downloading **158.**36
PEGI game classification system **121.**33
penalties
  cannabis cultivation **128.**31
  cannabis supply **128.**2, 9, 13
  drink-driving **143.**24
  for drug smuggling **163.**38
  possession of cannabis **128.**2, 9, 13, 27, 30, 31, 32
  underage sale of alcohol **143.**2
penalty notices **177.**8, 25
pensions **89.**23
  and civil partnerships **153.**28
  Europe **159.**25

gender gap **154**.6
saving for **134**.4, 25; **159**.21, 22; **180**.8
graduates **139**.36
UK **159**.3, 23, 25
universal social pension **159**.24
people-pleasing **170**.11
peptide hormones and analogues **118**.37
perception gap **170**.12
permissive parenting style **124**.8
personal crime, racial identity of victims **115**.10
personal information **168**.31
concerns about **168**.37
control of **158**.31-4
and Data Protection Act **168**.10-11
protecting **168**.31-2, 37
personal privacy **168**.31-9
personal skills gap **149**.37-8
personality and depression susceptibility **125**.2
pesco-vegetarian diet **140**.2
pester power **134**.12
pesticides **88**.13, 32, 34, 35
GM viruses **138**.13-14
petrol prices **119**.12-13, 14
see also fuel taxes
pets, death of **116**.13-14
PG film classification **121**.29
pharmaceutical industry **163**.1
and herbal medicine **81**.11
pharming **138**.4, 9-10, 20-22
hens for cancer treatment **138**.20-21
rice **138**.20
risks **138**.20, 21, 22
tobacco plants for HIV treatment **138**.21-2
phishing **134**.27-8, 28-9; **158**.33-4
phobias **141**.16-17
and young people **100**.2
phone bothering by parents **124**.15
physical abuse
bullying
children with learning diabilities **165**.15
disabled people **165**.17
of children **179**.1-2, 5

of older people **159**.16
signs of **179**.5
and stress **100**.1, 2
physical activity see exercise
physical punishment see corporal punishment
physician-assisted suicide (PAS) **152**.4, 7-8, 29-30, 31
see also assisted suicide
phytochemicals **88**.5, 7, 13
pica **127**.17
pill, contraceptive **176**.27
pink plateau **153**.39
pirate radio **142**.7
placebo effect, and complementary medicine **81**.26, 28, 34
plagiarism and the Internet **158**.2, 19-20
planning applications and sports facilities **118**.5
plants
endangered species **78**.2-3, 7
and photosynthesis **97**.9
in tropical rainforests **78**.11
see also genetically modified (GM) crops
plasmids **138**.2
plastic bags **161**.5, 13-14, 19, 36-7
plastic surgery see cosmetic surgery
plastic waste **161**.5, 22, 29
recycling **161**.24, 29
playground bullying and screen violence **121**.28
playgrounds for older people **159**.39
playing fields **118**.5-6
poisoning, first aid **136**.23
police **177**.33-4
arrest, your rights **128**.35-6; **177**.35-6
and asylum communities **89**.20
and beggars **130**.33
concerns about migrant crime **150**.12
domestic violence units **155**.29
and drugs offences **163**.38
and football hooliganism **118**.8
and online child pornography **99**.24
stop and search **177**.34
and Terrorism Act **147**.3
stop and search powers **147**.35-7
young people's attitudes to **177**.15-16

Volume numbers appear first (in bold) followed by page numbers; a change in volume number is preceded by a semi-colon.

Vol. 76 The Water Crisis
Vol. 78 Threatened Species
Vol. 81 Alternative Therapies
Vol. 88 Food and Nutrition
Vol. 89 Refugees
Vol. 97 Energy Matters
Vol. 99 Exploited Children
Vol. 100 Stress and Anxiety
Vol. 107 Work Issues
Vol. 116 Grief and Loss
Vol. 118 Focus on Sport
Vol. 119 Transport Trends
Vol. 121 The Censorship Debate
Vol. 124 Parenting Issues
Vol. 125 Understanding Depression
Vol. 127 Eating Disorders
Vol. 128 The Cannabis Issue
Vol. 129 Gambling Trends
Vol. 130 Homelessness
Vol. 133 Teen Pregnancy and Lone Parents
Vol. 134 Customers and Consumerism
Vol. 135 Coping with Disability
Vol. 136 Self-Harm

Vol. 138 A Genetically Modified Future?
Vol. 139 The Education Problem
Vol. 140 Vegetarian and Vegan Diets
Vol. 141 Mental Health
Vol. 142 Media Issues
Vol. 143 Problem Drinking
Vol. 144 The Cloning Debate
Vol. 145 Smoking Trends
Vol. 146 Sustainability and Environment
Vol. 147 The Terrorism Problem
Vol. 148 Religious Beliefs
Vol. 149 A Classless Society?
Vol. 150 Migration and Population
Vol. 151 Climate Change
Vol. 152 Euthanasia and the Right to Die
Vol. 153 Sexual Orientation and Society
Vol. 154 The Gender Gap
Vol. 155 Domestic Abuse
Vol. 156 Travel and Tourism
Vol. 157 The Problem of Globalisation
Vol. 158 The Internet Revolution
Vol. 159 An Ageing Population
Vol. 160 Poverty and Exclusion

Vol. 161 Waste Issues
Vol. 162 Staying Fit
Vol. 163 Drugs in the UK
Vol. 164 The AIDS Crisis
Vol. 165 Bullying Issues
Vol. 166 Marriage and Cohabitation
Vol. 167 Our Human Rights
Vol. 168 Privacy and Surveillance
Vol. 169 The Animal Rights Debate
Vol. 170 Body Image and Self-Esteem
Vol. 171 Abortion – Rights and Ethics
Vol. 172 Racial and Ethnic Discrimination
Vol. 173 Sexual Health
Vol. 174 Selling Sex
Vol. 175 Citizenship and Participation
Vol. 176 Health Issues for Young People
Vol. 177 Crime in the UK
Vol. 178 Reproductive Ethics
Vol. 179 Tackling Child Abuse
Vol. 180 Money and Finances
Vol. 181 The Housing Issue

political action and eating disorders 127.26
political media, women in 154.11
political and military globalisation 157.2
political overreaction to terrorism 147.10-11, 38-9
political parties 131.18
    housing policies 181.23
    views on hunting 169.28
    young peoples's support 131.32
political pressure on athletes 118.29
politics
    and competitive sport 118.4
    and free speech 121.7
    and genomics 138.3
    and gender equality 154.4, 6, 12, 21
    and human rights 167.4-5
    and the hunting debate 169.27-9
    and the media 142.2
    and newspapers 142.8
    older people's engagement in 159.7
    recommendations for change 131.25
    and support of media companies 121.5
    young people's involvement 131.27-35
    see also elections
pollution
    from aviation 119.16
    and endangered species 78.6
      in the UK 78.28, 29, 32
    and species extinction 78.11
    and transport 119.12, 13-14, 16, 30, 31; 146.35-6
      see also emissions, transport
    see also air pollution; water pollution
poorism (tourists visitng deprived areas) 156.33-5
population 150.28-39
    ageing population 159.3, 6
    and development goals 150.34
    global trends 150.34-5; 159.6
    information from census 150.36
    and poverty 150.34
    sustainable 150.31-2
population changes
    see ageing population; population growth
population control to combat climate change 151.31-2
population density and refugees 89.23
population growth 89.31
    and endangered species 78.1
    and the environment 146.12-13, 16-17; 150.27
    global 150.31, 32-3, 34
    and global water shortages 76.3, 5, 8, 15
    and immigration 150.16
    and water consumption 76.22, 29
    UK 150.28, 29, 31
pornography
    and the Internet 158.3
    R18 films 121.25, 20
    see also child pornography
port policing strategy, anti-terrorism 147.29
portage educational support 135.36
positive action and age discrimination 159.9-10
positive body image 170.17, 37
positive discrimination 154.36
positive thinking 141.36

as help for depression 125.3
possession of cannabis 128.2, 9, 13, 27, 30, 31, 32
postal voting 131.16
postcodes and population profiling 149.17
post-compulsory education 139.2
    see also A-levels; higher education; universities
post-mortem examination 116.32
post-natal depression 125.4, 17-18
    diagnosis of 125.17
    symptoms of 125.17
    treatment for 125.17-18
post-traumatic stress disorder (PTSD) 116.10; 141.3, 12; 176.30
potatoes, GM research trials 138.27, 28
poverty
    attitudes to 160.3, 4
    causes of 160.2, 25-6
    and child labour 99.2, 3, 4, 14-15
    children living in *see* child poverty
    children's perceptions of 149.9-12; 160.4
    and debt 160.12, 33
    definitions 160.1, 25, 26
    and disabled people 135.16-18; 160.10
    and education 160.16-22
    and environmental stress 146.16-17
    experiences of 160.13-14, 27
    extent of 160.1-2
    and free trade 157.9, 13, 26-7
    global 160.25-39
    and global financial crisis 180.1
    government action 160.21-2
    and government debt 157.9-10
    and health 149.14; 160.2
    and HIV/AIDS 96.24, 29; 164.10, 27
    impact of 160.2, 13-14
    measuring 160.1, 8
    and mental health problems 141.2, 22
    and Millennium Development Goals 160.30
    and older people 159.3
    and population 150.34
    and post traumatic stress disorder 141.3
    rich-poor gap
      global 160.26, 29
      UK 115.32; 149.19, 20, 22, 27, 29; 160.6, 7
    and segregation 115.30, 31, 32
    and the sexual exploitation of children 99.16, 24
    and smoking 145.21
    statistics 160.1-2, 25, 29
    and teenage pregnancy 133.20, 21
    in the UK 160.1-24
    and urbanization 150.38
    and water
      and development aid 76.30-1
      and human rights 76.25
      multinational water corporations 76.29
      supplies in developing countries 76.6
    and women 160.15
    see also child poverty; inequality
poverty line 160.1
power gap 154.4, 6
powers of dispersal 177.8
prayer 148.1

pre-implantation genetic diagnosis **144**.20; **178**.2, 28-9, 30-31, 31-2

pre-marital sex, attitudes to **166**.1

pre-paid cards **180**.26

pre-school children

    effects of divorce **124**.33

    gender differences **154**.24

    effects of poverty **160**.20

precursor cells **144**.25

pregnancy **178**.2-3

    and alcohol **143**.3, 25, 27, 33-4

    and domestic violence **155**.11, 30

    and exercise **162**.32

    and HIV **96**.16, 22, 23, 31, 38; **164**.3, 25, 27, 29-30, 31

    and male depression **125**.14

    planned, teenagers **133**.20

    and smoking **88**.7; **145**.32-3

    testing **133**.8

    see also abortion; teenage pregnancies

prejudice

    against bisexuals **153**.10

    and bullying **165**.8-9

    definition **115**.4

    against disabled people **135**.15, 30-31

    fears of parents of gay children **153**.9

    Islamaphobia **115**.36

    racial **131**.2

    religious **131**.3

    and sexual orientation **153**.2

    against transgender people **153**.13

    see also discrimination; homophobia

premature babies

    treatment decisions **152**.4, 32, 34

    viability **171**.23-4, 29, 31

prenatal screening **171**.22

prescription drugs, misuse **163**.14-16

press *see* media

Press Code **142**.26

press conferences **142**.12-13

press intrusion **168**.28-9

pressure on athletes to use drugs **118**.29

prices

alcohol, effect on consumption **143**.17, 31

cannabis **128**.2, 6

cigarettes **145**.17

    as deterrent to children smoking **145**.3

Primark and ethical trading **134**.30

primary age children, effects of divorce **124**.33

primary schools

    curriculum **139**.5, 6

    and gay issues **153**.19-20

    gender gap **154**.23

    and homophobic bullying **153**.15

    and pupils' mental health **141**.37

    see also schools

primates

    use in research **169**.24-6

    with jelly fish genes **144**.11

prison **177**.39

    prison leavers and homelessness **130**.11, 15

    prison sentences **177**.25, 37

        for cannabis possession **128**.13

        for knife crime **177**.38

    see also youth custody

privacy **168**.1-3, 28-30

    definition **168**.1

    legal rights **168**.1, 2-3

    and the media **142**.25, 26; 7, 28-9

    and National Identity Scheme **168**.15

    protection, models of **168**.2

    and social networking **168**.35-6

    see also freedom of information

privacy-invading software and domestic abuse **155**.15-16

private sales and consumer rights **134**.20

private schoolchildren

    attitudes to social differences **149**.9-12

    children's perceptions of **149**.11-12

private schools and university entrance **149**.34-5

privatisation

    and water management **76**.22-3, 32

        criticisms of private companies **76**.32

        multinational water corporations **76**.22, 23, 29-30

pro-abortion (pro-choice) arguments **171**.32-3

    presentations to schools **171**.38

Volume numbers appear first (in bold) followed by page numbers; a change in volume number is preceded by a semi-colon.

Vol. 76 The Water Crisis

Vol. 78 Threatened Species

Vol. 81 Alternative Therapies

Vol. 88 Food and Nutrition

Vol. 89 Refugees

Vol. 97 Energy Matters

Vol. 99 Exploited Children

Vol. 100 Stress and Anxiety

Vol. 107 Work Issues

Vol. 116 Grief and Loss

Vol. 118 Focus on Sport

Vol. 119 Transport Trends

Vol. 121 The Censorship Debate

Vol. 124 Parenting Issues

Vol. 125 Understanding Depression

Vol. 127 Eating Disorders

Vol. 128 The Cannabis Issue

Vol. 129 Gambling Trends

Vol. 130 Homelessness

Vol. 133 Teen Pregnancy and Lone Parents

Vol. 134 Customers and Consumerism

Vol. 135 Coping with Disability

Vol. 136 Self-Harm

Vol. 138 A Genetically Modified Future?

Vol. 139 The Education Problem

Vol. 140 Vegetarian and Vegan Diets

Vol. 141 Mental Health

Vol. 142 Media Issues

Vol. 143 Problem Drinking

Vol. 144 The Cloning Debate

Vol. 145 Smoking Trends

Vol. 146 Sustainability and Environment

Vol. 147 The Terrorism Problem

Vol. 148 Religious Beliefs

Vol. 149 A Classless Society?

Vol. 150 Migration and Population

Vol. 151 Climate Change

Vol. 152 Euthanasia and the Right to Die

Vol. 153 Sexual Orientation and Society

Vol. 154 The Gender Gap

Vol. 155 Domestic Abuse

Vol. 156 Travel and Tourism

Vol. 157 The Problem of Globalisation

Vol. 158 The Internet Revolution

Vol. 159 An Ageing Population

Vol. 160 Poverty and Exclusion

Vol. 161 Waste Issues

Vol. 162 Staying Fit

Vol. 163 Drugs in the UK

Vol. 164 The AIDS Crisis

Vol. 165 Bullying Issues

Vol. 166 Marriage and Cohabitation

Vol. 167 Our Human Rights

Vol. 168 Privacy and Surveillance

Vol. 169 The Animal Rights Debate

Vol. 170 Body Image and Self-Esteem

Vol. 171 Abortion – Rights and Ethics

Vol. 172 Racial and Ethnic Discrimination

Vol. 173 Sexual Health

Vol. 174 Selling Sex

Vol. 175 Citizenship and Participation

Vol. 176 Health Issues for Young People

Vol. 177 Crime in the UK

Vol. 178 Reproductive Ethics

Vol. 179 Tackling Child Abuse

Vol. 180 Money and Finances

Vol. 181 The Housing Issue

pro-life arguments **171**.21-3, 31
pro-life movement
  presentations to schools **171**.38
problem debt **134**.23
problem drinking *see* alcohol abuse
problem gambling *see* compulsive gambling
production, sustainable **146**.7, 8
prohibited steps order **166**.27, 35
promoters, sports, pressure on athletes to use drugs **118**.29
propaganda, terrorist, online **147**.8
property rights and cohabitation **166**.14
prostitution, children **167**.32
protectionism **157**.7, 13, 23-4
protectiveness, parental **124**.13-14
proteins **88**.6, 8
  definition **138**.4
  drugs produced by GM hens **138**.20-21
  teenage requirements **176**.8
  and vegan diet **140**.23-4
  and vegetarian diet **140**.3, 7
PSHE (personal, social and health education) **133**.16
psoriasis and smoking **145**.30
psychedelic drugs **163**.2, 6
psychiatric patients and smoking **145**.38
psychic prediction scams **134**.26
psychological abuse of older people **159**.16
psychological conditions and eating disorders **127**.9-10
psychological dependency on cannabis **128**.8
psychological effects
  of abortion **171**.9-10
  of nicotine **145**.26
psychologists, and young people and stress **100**.2
psychology
  of class **149**.6
  and gambling **129**.6, 29
  and religion **148**.12-13
psychosis **141**.1
  cannabis use **128**.15
psychosurgery **125**.26
psychotherapy
  and bipolar disorder **141**.14-15
  as a treatment for depression **125**.7, 26, 33
  and young people and stress **100**.2
PTSD (post-traumatic stress disorder) **116**.10; **141**.3, 12; **176**.30
puberty **127**.22
  and eating disorders **127**.2, 22-4
public attitudes
  to abortion **171**.8, 16, 30, 34
  to anti-terror measures **167**.24
  to biotechnology **138**.15-16; **144**.19
  to bullfighting **169**.38
  to cannabis use **128**.12
  to crime **177**.6, 23
  to euthanasia **152**.8, 12, 13, 15, 17
  to film classification **121**.24
  to the fur trade **169**.6
  to genetic modification **138**.3; **144**.20
  to human cloning **144**.35
  to human rights **167**.19
  to hunting with dogs **169**.29, 36
  to ID cards **168**.16

  to legal protection for gay people **153**.36
  to marriage and cohabitation **166**.1-2
  to mental ill-health **141**.25, 27
  to migrants **150**.3, 13-14, 17, 18-19
  to poverty **160**.3
  to refugees **89**.17
  to smacking **179**.32
  to smoking ban **145**.18
  terrorism fears **147**.12
public figures and privacy **168**.36
public grief **116**.17-18
public interest
  and journalists' rights **142**.27
  and media mergers **142**.4
public safety and censorship **121**.13
public service broadcasting, news coverage **142**.33
public services
  and gender equality **154**.3
  and National Identity Scheme **168**.16
public transport **119**.1, 12, 25
  and disabled people **135**.8
  encouraging use of **119**.39
  passes and personal data monitoring **168**.9
  usage **151**.39
punishment
  in schools, and racism **115**.19
  see also penalties
pupils, opinions on National Curriculum **139**.7
pupil referral units **135**.36

Q

qualifications **89**.34-5; **107**.1, 34; **139**.4
  and ethnicity **139**.8
  and gender **139**.10
  for university entrance **139**.29-30
  see also A-levels; AS-levels; degrees; educational
achievement; GCSEs
qualified human rights **167**.4
quality of goods, consumer rights **134**.2, 17
questioning by police **177**.35
quitting smoking *see* smoking, giving up
quotas for migrant workers **150**.7
quotations and consumer rights **134**.18

R

R18 film classification **121**.25, 30
rabbit-human embryos **144**.11
race
  and domestic violence **155**.4
  definition **115**.4
  as grounds for discrimination **115**.7
  names for **115**.4-5
race hate trials **121**.15
race relations **147**.19
racial background, UK population **115**.3, 24-5
racial discrimination **115**.4, 7-8
  and academic freedom **121**.8, 9

in employment **115**.13

see also racism

racial equality in football **118**.15-16

racial harassment

defining **115**.8

of refugees **89**.19, 20

racial identity

confusion over **149**.4

victims of crime **115**.10

racial integration **107**.12; **115**.6, 28-9; **131**.9; **147**.19

Asians **115**.37

in education **115**.29, 33

racial profiling and 'stop and search' **147**.35-6

racial segregation **115**.28-32

racially motivated crime **115**.9-10

racism **115**.1-2, 4

challenging **115**.2

and ChildLine **115**.1

and children **115**.9

defining **115**.4

and education **115**.19-20

effects of **115**.1

in football **118**.14

and Islamophobia **115**.36

laws **115**.2, 7-8, 11-12, 26

perception of **131**.2

reasons for **115**.1-2

in schools **115**.9, 19-20; **139**.9

in the workplace **115**.11-14

see also discrimination; employment and racism; ethnic minorities; racial discrimination

racist bullying **115**.2; **165**.9

racist incidents **115**.9

radio **158**.5, 6

interviews **142**.13-14

as news source **142**.33

pirate stations **142**.7

railways

congestion **119**.35

and disabled people **135**.8

travel trends **119**.1; **161**.31-2

rainfall and water distribution in the UK **76**.1-2

rainforests *see* forestry

rape

as reason for abortion **171**.21-2

as torture **167**.25-6

rate of return on education **139**.1, 37

reactive depression **125**.4

reality TV

breaking ethnic stereotypes **115**.22

and offensive language **121**.38-9

recession **180**.1-5

definition **180**.2

effects **180**.2

global **180**.1-2

indicators **180**.5

reclassification of cannabis **128**.13, 26-8, 29; **163**.32, 35-6

criticized **128**.38

effect on health **128**.30-32, 38

public attitudes to **128**.12

recombinant DNA technologies *see* genetic modification

recovered memory of sexual abuse **179**.26-9

recreational drugs use **163**.1

recruitment of employees, discrimination **115**.13

recycling **161**.2, 18, 19, 22-9

employment in **161**.2

increase in **161**.31

mobile phones **158**.13

negative effects **161**.35

organic waste *see* composting waste

organizations **161**.9

in public places **161**.20, 21

reducing emissions **161**.3

statistics **161**.22

targets **161**.20

redress (compensation) **134**.2, 17

reduce, reuse, recycle **161**.7, 18

reducing waste **161**.18

incentives for **161**.38

referral orders **177**.17, 31

reflexology **81**.3, 15-17, 23, 36

and stress-related illnesses **81**.16

training as a reflexologist **81**.16-17

refugees

Volume numbers appear first (in bold) followed by page numbers; a change in volume number is preceded by a semi-colon.

Vol. 76 The Water Crisis
Vol. 78 Threatened Species
Vol. 81 Alternative Therapies
Vol. 88 Food and Nutrition
Vol. 89 Refugees
Vol. 97 Energy Matters
Vol. 99 Exploited Children
Vol. 100 Stress and Anxiety
Vol. 107 Work Issues
Vol. 116 Grief and Loss
Vol. 118 Focus on Sport
Vol. 119 Transport Trends
Vol. 121 The Censorship Debate
Vol. 124 Parenting Issues
Vol. 125 Understanding Depression
Vol. 127 Eating Disorders
Vol. 128 The Cannabis Issue
Vol. 129 Gambling Trends
Vol. 130 Homelessness
Vol. 133 Teen Pregnancy and Lone Parents
Vol. 134 Customers and Consumerism
Vol. 135 Coping with Disability
Vol. 136 Self-Harm

Vol. 138 A Genetically Modified Future?
Vol. 139 The Education Problem
Vol. 140 Vegetarian and Vegan Diets
Vol. 141 Mental Health
Vol. 142 Media Issues
Vol. 143 Problem Drinking
Vol. 144 The Cloning Debate
Vol. 145 Smoking Trends
Vol. 146 Sustainability and Environment
Vol. 147 The Terrorism Problem
Vol. 148 Religious Beliefs
Vol. 149 A Classless Society?
Vol. 150 Migration and Population
Vol. 151 Climate Change
Vol. 152 Euthanasia and the Right to Die
Vol. 153 Sexual Orientation and Society
Vol. 154 The Gender Gap
Vol. 155 Domestic Abuse
Vol. 156 Travel and Tourism
Vol. 157 The Problem of Globalisation
Vol. 158 The Internet Revolution
Vol. 159 An Ageing Population
Vol. 160 Poverty and Exclusion

Vol. 161 Waste Issues
Vol. 162 Staying Fit
Vol. 163 Drugs in the UK
Vol. 164 The AIDS Crisis
Vol. 165 Bullying Issues
Vol. 166 Marriage and Cohabitation
Vol. 167 Our Human Rights
Vol. 168 Privacy and Surveillance
Vol. 169 The Animal Rights Debate
Vol. 170 Body Image and Self-Esteem
Vol. 171 Abortion – Rights and Ethics
Vol. 172 Racial and Ethnic Discrimination
Vol. 173 Sexual Health
Vol. 174 Selling Sex
Vol. 175 Citizenship and Participation
Vol. 176 Health Issues for Young People
Vol. 177 Crime in the UK
Vol. 178 Reproductive Ethics
Vol. 179 Tackling Child Abuse
Vol. 180 Money and Finances
Vol. 181 The Housing Issue

and homelessness 130.11-12, 19
    see also asylum seekers
refuges 155.12-13, 27-8, 32-3
regional differences
    disability 135.2
    smoking 145.1, 21
    social class 149.18
register of domestic violence offenders 155.39
register of GM land 138.19, 36
registering a death 116.31
regulation
    animal experiments 169.14, 20, 22
    of children's viewing 121.26-7
    of cloning 144.3
    of genetic modification 138.3, 11
    film 121.22-5, 29-30
    of hybrid embryo research 144.14
    media
        and civil liberties 142.1-2
        mergers 142.4
        online journalism 142.16
    stem cell cloning 144.27-8
    television 121.36-7
    video 121.26, 31
    video games 121.32-3
relational elements of marriage 166.2-3
relationships
    breakdown, and homelessness 130.3, 11, 15
    and cannabis use 128.9
    and depression, men 125.14
    dissolution 166.3
        see also divorce
    and football supporting 141.33
    and human cloning 144.6
    and mental health 141.34
    mixed-faith 115.39
    mixed-race 115.22-5
    and mobile phones 158.13
    problems 166.7-8
    teaching about relationships 170.14
    teenage, and violence 179.19
relaxation
    and depression 125.39
    and stress 100.29-30, 31-2, 34, 36-7
released (outdoor) GMOs 138.12
relief, feelings after bereavement 116.4, 19
religion 148.1-39
    and abortion 171.17-19
    and abortion education 171.39
    attitudes to 148.26, 27
    and attitudes to animals 169.2
    and the Census (2001) 148.6-7
    and corporal punishment 179.36
    and euthanasia 152.7, 11, 12, 15, 34
    and food rules 148.10-11
    functions 148.1
    funeral traditions 116.33-5
    and the law 148.29
    and moral decline 148.17
    religious observance in Britain 148.6-8, 18-19, 25, 27
    religious tolerance 148.23-39

surveys 148.8, 27
    and terrorism 147.1
    theories of 148.12-13
    women in the workforce 154.29
    see also individual religions
religious discrimination 115.26; 148.28, 29
religious groups
    and disability 135.2
    segregation 115.32
religious identity 115.5, 26
religious marriage ceremonies 166.6
religious prejudice, perception of 131.3
religiously motivated crime 115.27; 148.29
    terrorism 147.1, 5
religious texts 148.1
religious values 148.16
remembrance of the deceased 116.16-17, 20, 24
    remembrance book 116.16
    remembrance ceremonies 116.23
    remembrance services 116.17
remittances from migrants 150.2
remote gambling 129.17-26
remote sensing 168.26-7
renewable energy 97.6-18, 26; 151.29-30
    advantages of 97.9
    attitudes to 97.5
    bioenergy 97.5, 6, 9, 11, 18
    case for 97.1-2, 6-7
    costs of 97.19, 38
    defining 97.8-9
    electricity from 97.4, 11, 37-8
    future of 97.8-9
    hydroelectric power 97.4, 5, 6, 12, 14, 38
    and nuclear power 97.6, 7, 19, 21
    sources of 97.4
    types of 97.9
    in the UK 97.13-14, 26, 39
    see also energy efficiency; solar energy; wind energy
rent deposit schemes 130.29
rented accommodation
    as alternative to selling 181.17
    shortage 130.8
    support services 130.29
    young people 181.26, 33
reparation orders 177.17, 31
repayment mortgages 181.28
repossessed homes websites 181.7
reproductive cloning 144.15; 178.36, 37
    see also human reproductive cloning
reproductive rights, disabled people 135.27
reproductive system, effects of eating disorders 127.5
reprogrammed cells 144.26
residence of children after divorce 166.35
residential mobility 149.26
resin, cannabis (hashish) 128.1, 3, 6, 23
    seizures of 128.31
resources
    natural 146.9
    resource efficiency 146.7
respiratory health
    and cannabis 128.18-19

lung cancer **128**.17, 19, 28; **145**.34
   and passive smoking **145**.29
responsibility, encouraging children's **124**.13-14
responsible drinking **143**.26-7, 29
responsible travel **134**.30; **156**.1, 20-39
   definition **156**.24
   see also ecotourism
restaurants
   and vegans **140**.25
   and vegetarians **140**.5
restorative justice **177**.31
retail industry **107**.5
   and environmentalism **146**.38
   packaging waste **161**.12
   plastic bags **161**.13-14
retirement
   age of **107**.13
   feelings about **159**.15
   and male depression **125**.15
   retiring abroad **150**.24
   saving for **159**.21, 22; **180**.8
   spending patterns, retired people **159**.19
   working after retirement age **159**.10, 15
   see also pensions
reusing goods **161**.18
reverse anorexia **127**.19
rice, GM contamination **138**.20, 31-4
rich-poor gap
   global **160**.26, 29
   UK **115**.32; **149**.19, 20, 22, 27, 29; **160**.6, 7
'right to buy' scheme, social housing **181**.25
right to move, council tenants **181**.35-6
right-wing terrorism **147**.1
rights
   in abortion
      of doctors **171**.27-28
      of the fetus **171**.17
      of women **171**.17, 20
   on arrest **177**.35-6
   children's *see* children's rights
   consumer *see* consumer rights
   of migrant workers **150**.2

to protest **121**.14
   about offensive material **121**.13
to privacy **168**.2-3
young people **167**.28-39
see also human rights
rivers
   drying up of **76**.2, 35
   pollution **76**.4
      and freshwater supplies **76**.15
   and species extinction **78**.10
road accidents **119**.4, 5, 28, 30-31
   and children **119**.5, 28, 30-31
   deaths **119**.4, 5, 28, 30
   and speed **119**.5, 30-31
   see also drink-driving
road building to ease congestion **119**.12
road charging **119**.35, 36
   congestion charging **119**.12, 34-5, 38
road safety **119**.4
   education **119**.5-6
   quiz **119**.6
road traffic **119**.1
   carbon offsetting **151**.22
   increase **119**.11, 13, 29
   injuries, children **119**.5, 28, 30-31
   pollution *see* pollution and transport
   see also cars
Roman Catholics *see* Catholic Church
rough sleeping **130**.9-12
   Scotland **130**.6
   see also homelessness
round-the-world tickets **156**.15
RSPCA Freedom Food mark **140**.29, 34
rubbish *see* waste
running, effect on joints **162**.33
rural districts *see* countryside
Rwanda, human rights abuses **167**.13

S

SAD (Seasonal Affective Disorder) **125**.4, 18, 37-8; **141**.35

Volume numbers appear first (in bold) followed by page numbers; a change in volume number is preceded by a semi-colon.

Vol. 76 The Water Crisis
Vol. 78 Threatened Species
Vol. 81 Alternative Therapies
Vol. 88 Food and Nutrition
Vol. 89 Refugees
Vol. 97 Energy Matters
Vol. 99 Exploited Children
Vol. 100 Stress and Anxiety
Vol. 107 Work Issues
Vol. 116 Grief and Loss
Vol. 118 Focus on Sport
Vol. 119 Transport Trends
Vol. 121 The Censorship Debate
Vol. 124 Parenting Issues
Vol. 125 Understanding Depression
Vol. 127 Eating Disorders
Vol. 128 The Cannabis Issue
Vol. 129 Gambling Trends
Vol. 130 Homelessness
Vol. 133 Teen Pregnancy and Lone Parents
Vol. 134 Customers and Consumerism
Vol. 135 Coping with Disability
Vol. 136 Self-Harm

Vol. 138 A Genetically Modified Future?
Vol. 139 The Education Problem
Vol. 140 Vegetarian and Vegan Diets
Vol. 141 Mental Health
Vol. 142 Media Issues
Vol. 143 Problem Drinking
Vol. 144 The Cloning Debate
Vol. 145 Smoking Trends
Vol. 146 Sustainability and Environment
Vol. 147 The Terrorism Problem
Vol. 148 Religious Beliefs
Vol. 149 A Classless Society?
Vol. 150 Migration and Population
Vol. 151 Climate Change
Vol. 152 Euthanasia and the Right to Die
Vol. 153 Sexual Orientation and Society
Vol. 154 The Gender Gap
Vol. 155 Domestic Abuse
Vol. 156 Travel and Tourism
Vol. 157 The Problem of Globalisation
Vol. 158 The Internet Revolution
Vol. 159 An Ageing Population
Vol. 160 Poverty and Exclusion

Vol. 161 Waste Issues
Vol. 162 Staying Fit
Vol. 163 Drugs in the UK
Vol. 164 The AIDS Crisis
Vol. 165 Bullying Issues
Vol. 166 Marriage and Cohabitation
Vol. 167 Our Human Rights
Vol. 168 Privacy and Surveillance
Vol. 169 The Animal Rights Debate
Vol. 170 Body Image and Self-Esteem
Vol. 171 Abortion – Rights and Ethics
Vol. 172 Racial and Ethnic Discrimination
Vol. 173 Sexual Health
Vol. 174 Selling Sex
Vol. 175 Citizenship and Participation
Vol. 176 Health Issues for Young People
Vol. 177 Crime in the UK
Vol. 178 Reproductive Ethics
Vol. 179 Tackling Child Abuse
Vol. 180 Money and Finances
Vol. 181 The Housing Issue

safe sex **176**.22, 27, 28

safety
of abortion **171**.3, 4, 11-12
and alcoholic drinks labelling **143**.30, 31, 32
and cycling **119**.28
and gender equality **154**.3-4, 6
of genetically modified crops **138**.6-6, 24
of goods, consumer rights **134**.20
and mobile phones **158**.13
parents' fears **124**.13-14
transport **119**.1
and walking to school **119**.26
at work **107**.31

safety and the Internet **165**.26-7, 30-31
children and young people **158**.27-30
online shopping **158**.31
social networking **158**.9, 10-11; **179**.18

salaries
graduates **139**.35, 36, 37
teachers **139**.12
young people's expectations **180**.21-2
see also earnings; wages

salmonella **88**.28

salt intake **88**.2, 7, 10, 16, 23, 26

same-sex relationships
and domestic abuse **155**.13-15
having a child **178**.9-10

sanitation
in developing countries **76**.7, 8, 12, 17, 21; **146**.14-15
and the right to water **76**.24

Sarah's Law, dangers of **179**.20-21

satellite surveillance **168**.26-7

saturated fats **88**.2, 22-3

savings
for old age **159**.21, 22; **180**.8
levels of **134**.25; **180**.7
savings accounts **180**.26
savings ratio **180**.7
and social class **149**.20

saviour siblings **178**.28-31

scabies **96**.7

scalds, first aid **136**.23

scams **134**.26-9

schizophrenia **141**.4-5
and cannabis use **128**.14-15

school bullying
anti-bullying policies **165**.1, 8, 25
and film violence **121**.28

school leavers, lack of basic skills **139**.17

school leaving age **139**.1, 26

schools
abortion information **171**.36-9
absences, gender differences **154**.25
academies **139**.14-16
alcohol education in **143**.20
anti-bullying policies **165**.1, 8, 25
biometric fingerprinting **168**.30
and CCTV **168**.25
and children in developing countries **76**.13-14
citizenship teaching **131**.36
costs **160**.16-17, 18, 19

and cyberbullying **165**.24-7, 29
and drugs **163**.28-9
and disabled children **135**.24-5
and emergency planning **147**.31-2
and ethnic minority children **115**.18, 19-21
exclusions, gender differences **154**.24
faith-based **148**.34, 35-6
and financial education **180**.38-9
and global citizenship **131**.37
and homophobia **153**.14-18
intake, effect on attainment **149**.31-3
and integration **115**.29, 33
intelligent design, teaching **148**.39
journeys to **119**.25, 26-7, 29-30
and mental health education **141**.37
multi-faith **148**.32-3
and physical activity **162**.13
private, and university entrance **149**.34-5
and physical activity **162**.13
pupil-teacher ratio **139**.12
and racism **115**.9, 19-20
self-harm support **136**.11, 18
sex education *see* sex education
single-sex **139**.11-12
and special educational needs **135**.36-9
sports **118**.3, 4
statistics **139**.1
and stress **100**.1; **176**.37, 38-9
and university entrance **149**.34-5
weighing children **127**.36; **162**.16
workforce, gender differences **154**.25
young people and stress **100**.1
see also education; National Curriculum; primary schools;
secondary schools

science education
A-level choices **139**.21-2
gender differences **154**.22-3

scientific research, and animal experiments **169**.14-26

Scotland
age of consent **133**.1
biodiversity threats **146**.21
children and gambling **129**.32-3
and euthanasia legislation **152**.17, 29, 30
feelings of Scottish identity **131**.5
homelessness **130**.5-6, 13
self-harm by older people **136**.20
suicides **136**.34, 35
teenage abortion **133**.2
teenage pregnancy **133**.2, 5, 19

scratchcards and under 16s **129**.12

screen violence, influence on children **121**.28, 33, 34, 35

scriptures **148**.1

sea level rise **151**.8; **157**.2

seafood, sustainable **146**.29

search engines **158**.2, 25-6

Seasonal Affective Disorder (SAD) **125**.4, 18, 37-8; **141**.35

seasonal labour **89**.22-3

second-hand goods, consumer rights **134**.2

second-hand smoke *see* passive smoking

secondary schools
curriculum **139**.5-6

see also A-levels; GCSEs; schools
security, national **147**.2-3
security alerts **147**.30
segregation **115**.28-32
segregation indices **115**.31-2
selective breeding **138**.12
Selective Serotonin Re-uptake Inhibitors (SSRIs) **125**.8, 10, 32
selenium
 in red meat **140**.12
 and vegetarian diets **140**.7
self-acceptance **170**.8-9
self-affirmation **170**.38
self-blame *see* blame, feelings of
self build projects **181**.30-31
self-censorship, broadcasters **121**.36-7
self-directed violence *see* self-harm; suicide
self-employment **107**.2
self-esteem **127**.24; **170**.1-16
 assessing your self-esteem **170**.4-5
 and body image **170**.19
 changes over lifetime **170**.16
 children **170**.9-10
 damaging experiences **170**.8
 definition **170**.1-2
 effects of bullying **165**.16
 and eating disorders **127**.2
 high, problems of **170**.13
 improving **136**.3, **170**.1, 2, 3, 8-9
  through learning and skills development **130**.35
  children **170**.9-10
 questionnaire **170**.4-5
 sources of **170**.8
 and sport **170**.39
self-harm **136**.1-26; **176**.30, 33-5
 age of self-harmers **136**.4, 20
 asking for help **136**.12-13, 21
 case studies **136**.6, 15-16
 as coping strategy **136**.10, 25
 definition **136**.1, 4, 10, 17, 24
 and eating disorders **127**.10
 as expression of feelings **136**.10, 18
 in groups **136**.8-9

methods of **136**.1, 7, 9, 17, 26
minimizing damage **136**.22-3
myths about **136**.8-9
older people **136**.20
peer support **136**.18
prevalence **136**.4, 7, 10
prevention **136**.4-5
risk factors **136**.2, 10
signs **136**.9, 10-11
sources of help **136**.3, 12-13, 21
self-help **136**.3, 19, 21
stopping **136**.3, 21
and suicide **136**.2, 9, 11, 24-6
treatment **136**.11
young people **136**.2, 4-19; **176**.33-5
self help housing **181**.32
self-image *see* body image
self-injury **136**.1-26
self-poisoning **136**.26
semantic web **158**.25-6
semen and fertility problems **178**.4-5
sensory impairment and age **159**.4
sentencing **177**.24-6
 community sentencing **177**.24, 25-9
 knife crime **177**.38-9
 youth courts **177**.17-18
separation
 effect on children **124**.33-4; **166**.4-5, 29-31, 32
 and male depression **125**.14
 see also divorce
serotonin **141**.9
 and eating disorders **127**.6-7
services and child labour **99**.2, 4
sex, definition **154**.1
sex discrimination **154**.6
 in the workplace **154**.30
  see also glass ceiling, pay gap
 worldwide **154**.13-14
sex education **133**.12-16
 age of children **133**.15
 aims **133**.13
 and attitudes to sex **133**.14

Volume numbers appear first (in bold) followed by page numbers; a change in volume number is preceded by a semi-colon.

Vol. 76 The Water Crisis
Vol. 78 Threatened Species
Vol. 81 Alternative Therapies
Vol. 88 Food and Nutrition
Vol. 89 Refugees
Vol. 97 Energy Matters
Vol. 99 Exploited Children
Vol. 100 Stress and Anxiety
Vol. 107 Work Issues
Vol. 116 Grief and Loss
Vol. 118 Focus on Sport
Vol. 119 Transport Trends
Vol. 121 The Censorship Debate
Vol. 124 Parenting Issues
Vol. 125 Understanding Depression
Vol. 127 Eating Disorders
Vol. 128 The Cannabis Issue
Vol. 129 Gambling Trends
Vol. 130 Homelessness
Vol. 133 Teen Pregnancy and Lone Parents
Vol. 134 Customers and Consumerism
Vol. 135 Coping with Disability
Vol. 136 Self-Harm

Vol. 138 A Genetically Modified Future?
Vol. 139 The Education Problem
Vol. 140 Vegetarian and Vegan Diets
Vol. 141 Mental Health
Vol. 142 Media Issues
Vol. 143 Problem Drinking
Vol. 144 The Cloning Debate
Vol. 145 Smoking Trends
Vol. 146 Sustainability and Environment
Vol. 147 The Terrorism Problem
Vol. 148 Religious Beliefs
Vol. 149 A Classless Society?
Vol. 150 Migration and Population
Vol. 151 Climate Change
Vol. 152 Euthanasia and the Right to Die
Vol. 153 Sexual Orientation and Society
Vol. 154 The Gender Gap
Vol. 155 Domestic Abuse
Vol. 156 Travel and Tourism
Vol. 157 The Problem of Globalisation
Vol. 158 The Internet Revolution
Vol. 159 An Ageing Population
Vol. 160 Poverty and Exclusion

Vol. 161 Waste Issues
Vol. 162 Staying Fit
Vol. 163 Drugs in the UK
Vol. 164 The AIDS Crisis
Vol. 165 Bullying Issues
Vol. 166 Marriage and Cohabitation
Vol. 167 Our Human Rights
Vol. 168 Privacy and Surveillance
Vol. 169 The Animal Rights Debate
Vol. 170 Body Image and Self-Esteem
Vol. 171 Abortion – Rights and Ethics
Vol. 172 Racial and Ethnic Discrimination
Vol. 173 Sexual Health
Vol. 174 Selling Sex
Vol. 175 Citizenship and Participation
Vol. 176 Health Issues for Young People
Vol. 177 Crime in the UK
Vol. 178 Reproductive Ethics
Vol. 179 Tackling Child Abuse
Vol. 180 Money and Finances
Vol. 181 The Housing Issue

and magazines **142**.28, 29
role of parents **133**.12, 15
sex offenders
disclosure of **179**.20-21
help for **179**.22-3
sex offenders notification **177**.18
travel restriction **156**.37
Sex and Relationships Education (SRE) **133**.12-13
sex tourism **156**.37-9
sex work and street lifestyle **130**.12
sexist bullying **165**.9, 10-11, 12-14
sexual abuse **179**.2-3, 13-29
and child domestic workers **99**.8, 9
effects **179**.24-5
false memories **179**.26-9
getting help **179**.25
and the Internet **179**.15-17
of older people **159**.16-17
signs of **179**.5
statistics **179**.13, 15, 17
and stress **100**.1, 2
sexual abusers *see* paedophiles; sex offenders
sexual behaviour
and HIV **96**.12, 14, 16, 17
and male depression **125**.14
and sexually transmitted infections **96**.9, 12
teenagers **133**.1-3
sexual exploitation of children **99**.1, 4, 16-18, 20-8; **167**.22
case studies **99**.21-2
harmful effects of **99**.16, 20
and poverty **99**.16, 24
and sex tourism **156**.37-9
teenagers **99**.20-2
and trafficking **99**.3, 16, 17, 18, 20, 21, 24, 28
see also child pornography; child prostitution
sexual health **176**.21-8
being ready for sex **176**.21-2
and migrants **150**.21-3
safe sex **176**.22, 27, 28
sexual dysfunction **176**.23
see also contraception; sexually transmitted infections
sexual identity confusion **149**.5
sexual imagery and TV watershed **121**.38
sexual offences prevention order **177**.18
sexual orientation **153**.1-25
and bullying **165**.2, 9, 12-14
causes **153**.2, 6, 7
definition **153**.1
discovering **153**.1-2, 4, 7, 12
and the law **153**.26-39
modification therapy **153**.3
prejudice **153**.2-3
survey **153**.5
sexualisation of young girls **154**.10
sexuality *see* sexual orientation
sexually transmitted infections (STIs) **96**.1-13; **176**.23, 24-8
avoiding **96**.1-2; **176**.24, 26
bacterial **96**.3, 10, 12
chlamydia **96**.2-3, 4, 5, 8, 10, 12; **176**.25, 26
effects on fertility **178**.5
genital herpes **96**.3, 4, 6, 10, 12

genital warts **96**.2-3, 4, 5-6, 12-13
gonorrhoea **96**.2, 3, 4, 5, 8, 10, 12
and HIV **96**.10, 12, 25
increase in **96**.4
pubic lice **96**.7
and sexual behaviour **96**.9, 12
symptoms of **96**.1, 5, 6, 7
syphilis **96**.3, 4, 6, 8, 10, 12
testing for **96**.1, 2, 3, 5, 6, 7, 10
treatment of **96**.1, 5, 6, 7, 10
trichomonas vaginalis **96**.6-7
types of **96**.2
in the UK **96**.2-3, 4
viral **96**.12-13
and young people **96**.3, 4, 8-9; **133**.2-3, 12-13, 17; **176**.25, 26, 28
see also Genito-Urinary Medicine (GUM) clinics
shared accommodation, and planning policy **181**.19-20
shared ownership homes **181**.25, 31
shock as response to bereavement **116**.3-4
shoes, recycling **161**.28
shopping
addiction to **134**.13, 14
and animal welfare **140**.31, 33
and children **134**.12
and energy efficiency **97**.31-2
Internet **134**.15-16; **158**.3, 30-31
as social experience for women **134**.16
see also consumer rights; consumerism; consumers
shouting as form of child abuse **179**.39
siblings
donor siblings **178**.26-7
saviour siblings **178**.28-31
sibling trouble **124**.18
sickness absence **107**.6-8; **154**.18
Sikhism **148**.5
and faith schools **148**.35
festivals **148**.5
food rules **148**.5
funerals **116**.34
simple carbohydrates **88**.2
single homelessness **130**.1-2
single parents *see* lone parents
single-sex education **139**.11-12; **154**.25, 26, 27
single-sex youth work **154**.5
sinsemilla (cannabis) **128**.1, 4
size-related bullying **165**.8-9
size zero **170**.20
skills shortages **107**.31-3
skin, effects of smoking **145**.30
skin cancer **176**.10-11
skunk (cannabis) **128**.2, 3-4, 13
home growing **128**.3-4, 30-31
mental health effects **128**.15
slander **142**.26
slavery **167**.20-22
Britain **167**.21, 22
children **99**.1; **167**.32-3
statistics **167**.20
sleep
and exercise **141**.39

and mental health **141**.34
and stress **100**.19, 27, 29
sleeping rough *see* rough sleeping
slum tours **156**.33-5
smacking children **167**.36-9
   arguments against ban **167**.39; **179**.33
   and human rights **167**.36-8; **179**.30, 31-2
   public opinion **179**.32
   see also corporal punishment
smallpox vaccinations **147**.31
smoking
   age of smokers **145**.1
   anti-smoking advertising **145**.18-19
   ban on smoking in public places *see* smoking ban
   cannabis **128**.8
      effects of **128**.5, 18-19
   children **145**.2-3; **176**.3, 12-13
      attitudes to smoking **145**.20
      and the law **176**.13
      starting smoking **176**.12
   costs of **145**.17, 38
      as deterrent **145**.3; **176**.13
   deaths from **145**.1, 4, 12, 22, 24; **163**.11
   effects on appearance **176**.11
   effects on fertility **178**.5
   giving up **145**.33, 35-9
      benefits **145**.27, 35
      numbers of people giving up **145**.1
      reasons for giving up **145**.15
   and health **145**.25-39
      benefits of giving up **145**.27, 35
      children **145**.2; **176**.12-13
      developing countries **145**.23
   and life expectancy **145**.21
   men **145**.21, 22
      and fertility **145**.32
   passive smoking **145**.2, 28-9
   statistics **145**.1, 3, 4
   and stress **100**.19, 27, 31, 34, 35, 37
   withdrawal symptoms **145**.26-7
   women **145**.21, 22
      and fertility **145**.32

   workplace smoking ban **145**.14
   young people **145**.3, 4; **176**.4, 12-13
      influence of films on smoking habits **145**.9-10
      and the law **145**.3
      prevention **176**.13
      reasons for smoking **145**.5
smoking ban (ban on smoking in public places) **145**.11-17
   effect on mental health staff **145**.39
   effect on mental health sufferers **145**.38-9
   effect on pubs **145**.13
   effect on tobacco industry **145**.16-17
   legal challenge **145**.15
   public attitudes **145**.13, 18
   and workplaces **145**.14
soaps, TV
   and offensive language **121**.38
   and teenage drinking **143**.18-19
social care services
   and disabled people **135**.4
   expectations of **135**.18
   insufficiency **135**.20
   and older people **159**.4, 28, 26, 29
social class **149**.1-17
   and advertising **134**.8
   and attitudes to money **149**.19-20
   and attitudes to moving home **149**.26
   and children's nutrition **162**.13-14
   classification **149**.3, 5
   confusion over **149**.4
   and educational attainment **149**.30, 31-3; **154**.23
   gender and pupil behaviour **154**.24-5
   and mental health problems **141**.2
   and obesity **162**.5
   psychology of **149**.6
   regional differences **149**.18
   self-awareness of **149**.3, 4, 18, 19, 24
   see also social mobility
social and cultural globalisation **157**.2
social differences, children's perceptions of **149**.9-12
social exclusion
   and education **160**.17-18
   older people **159**.30

Volume numbers appear first (in bold) followed by page numbers; a change in volume number is preceded by a semi-colon.

Vol. 76 The Water Crisis
Vol. 78 Threatened Species
Vol. 81 Alternative Therapies
Vol. 88 Food and Nutrition
Vol. 89 Refugees
Vol. 97 Energy Matters
Vol. 99 Exploited Children
Vol. 100 Stress and Anxiety
Vol. 107 Work Issues
Vol. 116 Grief and Loss
Vol. 118 Focus on Sport
Vol. 119 Transport Trends
Vol. 121 The Censorship Debate
Vol. 124 Parenting Issues
Vol. 125 Understanding Depression
Vol. 127 Eating Disorders
Vol. 128 The Cannabis Issue
Vol. 129 Gambling Trends
Vol. 130 Homelessness
Vol. 133 Teen Pregnancy and Lone Parents
Vol. 134 Customers and Consumerism
Vol. 135 Coping with Disability
Vol. 136 Self-Harm

Vol. 138 A Genetically Modified Future?
Vol. 139 The Education Problem
Vol. 140 Vegetarian and Vegan Diets
Vol. 141 Mental Health
Vol. 142 Media Issues
Vol. 143 Problem Drinking
Vol. 144 The Cloning Debate
Vol. 145 Smoking Trends
Vol. 146 Sustainability and Environment
Vol. 147 The Terrorism Problem
Vol. 148 Religious Beliefs
Vol. 149 A Classless Society?
Vol. 150 Migration and Population
Vol. 151 Climate Change
Vol. 152 Euthanasia and the Right to Die
Vol. 153 Sexual Orientation and Society
Vol. 154 The Gender Gap
Vol. 155 Domestic Abuse
Vol. 156 Travel and Tourism
Vol. 157 The Problem of Globalisation
Vol. 158 The Internet Revolution
Vol. 159 An Ageing Population
Vol. 160 Poverty and Exclusion

Vol. 161 Waste Issues
Vol. 162 Staying Fit
Vol. 163 Drugs in the UK
Vol. 164 The AIDS Crisis
Vol. 165 Bullying Issues
Vol. 166 Marriage and Cohabitation
Vol. 167 Our Human Rights
Vol. 168 Privacy and Surveillance
Vol. 169 The Animal Rights Debate
Vol. 170 Body Image and Self-Esteem
Vol. 171 Abortion – Rights and Ethics
Vol. 172 Racial and Ethnic Discrimination
Vol. 173 Sexual Health
Vol. 174 Selling Sex
Vol. 175 Citizenship and Participation
Vol. 176 Health Issues for Young People
Vol. 177 Crime in the UK
Vol. 178 Reproductive Ethics
Vol. 179 Tackling Child Abuse
Vol. 180 Money and Finances
Vol. 181 The Housing Issue

social factors and gambling **129.**7, 29
social gambling **129.**11, 18
social group classification system **149.**3, 5
social housing
    attitudes to **181.**14
    and children **181.**9-11
    demand for **181.**29
    effects of **181.**9-11; 33-5
    government strategy **130.**16, 33
    and immigrants **181.**12
    quality **181.**10
    shortage **130.**8, 23; **181.**8
social inclusion effects of homelessness, children **130.**23
social isolation
    Asians **115.**37
    older people **159.**3, 8, 17, 30
    and self-harm **136.**18
social mobility **160.**7
    and education **139.**13; **149.**22, 25, 30, 36-7
    international comparisons **149.**25
social model of disability **135.**1
social networking **142.**35, 36, 38; **158.**3, 9
    and globalisation **157.**15
    and mobile phones **158.**11-12
    and privacy **168.**34-6
    safety **158.**9, 10-11; **179.**18
    and travel **156.**14
    and workplace bullying **165.**37-8
social pessimism **177.**1-4
social pressures
    on athletes to use drugs **118.**29
    and eating disorders **127.**2
social problems, public perceptions of **177.**1-4
social profiles by neighbourhood **149.**17, 23
social responsibility, corporate **157.**11
social roles and gender differences **154.**9
social security benefits *see* state benefits
social skills gap **149.**37-8
social status and ageing **159.**32
social topography **149.**17, 23
social workers
    and stress in young people **100.**2
    and workplace stress **100.**12
socio-economic deprivation, migrants **150.**22
socio-economic groups
    and disability **135.**2
    and news awareness **142.**31
    and non-traditional families **124.**21
    and obesity **162.**5
    and smoking **145.**1, 21
    see also social class
soft segregation **115.**28
soft skills (emotional skills) **170.**5
solar activity and global warming **151.**5-6
solar energy **97.**2, 4, 6, 8-9, 10, 21
    costs of **97.**14
    and energy efficiency **97.**31
    market for **97.**14
    PV (Photovoltaics) **97.**8, 9, 12, 13, 38
    in the UK **97.**10, 13, 14, 26
soldiers

    child *see* child soldiers
    suicides, Japan **136.**39
solicitors
    and divorce **166.**35
    and mediation **166.**39
solid fuels, as a source of energy **97.**4
solvent abuse **163.**5-6
    deaths from **163.**11
somatic-cell nuclear transfer (SCNT) **144.**1-2, 9, 26
    see also therapeutic cloning
soup runs **130.**31
souvenirs, wildlife **156.**32
soya products for vegetarians **140.**22, 23, 26
spa holidays 5
space
    as a natural resource **146.**9
    sustainable use of **146.**17
Special Educational Needs (SEN) **135.**36-9
    gender differences **154.**24
    and mainstream schooling **135.**37-9
special schools **135.**36
specialist diplomas **139.**23-5
species boundaries **144.**12
specific issue order **166.**27, 35
spectacles, recycling **161.**28
spectators, pressure on athletes to use drugs **118.**23
speed cameras **119.**4, 17, 18
speed limiters **119.**18
speed limits
    and active traffic management **119.**37-8
    raising **119.**4
speeding **119.**3, 4, 8
    and pedestrian injuries **119.**5, 30-31
spending **134.**3-4; **180.**7
    on advertising **134.**7
    and budgeting **180.**30-31
    on credit cards **134.**24
    on education **139.**1
    on ethical products **134.**31, 32
    older people **159.**19
    on tourism **156.**5, 10
    see also consumer spending
sperm cell creation
    from bone marrow **144.**29
    from stem cells **178.**39
sperm donation **178.**10-12
    concerns about **178.**12
    donor contact with offspring **178.**25-7
    effects of removing donor anonymity **178.**24
spin, government **121.**17-18
spin doctors **131.**18
spinal damage, stem cell therapy **144.**21
spirits, strength of **143.**1
spirituality **148.**1
    interest in **148.**19
sponsorship and women's sport **118.**21
sport
    betting **129.**2
    and drugs **118.**23-39
    and inclusion **118.**12-22
    participation *see* participation in sport

and self-esteem **170**.39
trends **118**.1-11
sports facilities **118**.5-6
spot-reduction of fat **162**.33
spread betting **129**.2
spyware **158**.34
and domestic abuse **155**.15-16
squatting **181**.20
SSRIs (Selective Serotonin Re-Uptake Inhibitors) **125**.8, 10, 32
St John's wort, treatment for Seasonal Affective Disorder **125**.37-8
stamp duty **181**.24
political party policies **181**.23
standing orders **180**.14
Staphylococcus aureus **88**.29
starchy foods **88**.5-6, 12
state benefits **160**.23-4
for asylum seekers **89**.12, 13, 14, 19, 30, 38
benefit problems
and debt **130**.25
and homelessness **130**.9, 12
after bereavement **116**.30
Child Tax Credit **133**.33
costs of incapacity benefit **100**.23
Council Tax Benefit, lone parents **133**.35, 38
disabled people **135**.3, 4, 5-6
low take-up **135**.18
Housing Benefit **133**.34-5
problems, and homelessness **130**.9
jobseekers' allowance **100**.23
and lone parents **133**.33-6, 37, 38
amount discrepancies **133**.36
encouraging single parenthood **133**.32
and migrants **150**.7
and National Identity Scheme **168**.16, 18
Working Tax Credit **133**.35
see also disability benefits
state pension **159**.3, 23
state religion **148**.21-2
statutory homelessness **130**.2-3, 13
steel cans recycling **161**.27
stem cell lines **144**.18

personalized **144**.25
stem cell research **144**.2, 15-29; **178**.38
embryonic **178**.33-7
ethical issues **144**.6, 17; **178**.33-5
how it works **144**.16
humanist view **178**.36-7
induced pluripotent stem cells **178**.38
public attitudes to **138**.16; **144**.19
timeline **144**.27-8, 33
using hybrid embryos **144**.14
stem cell therapy **144**.17-18, 21-6, 28
stem cell transplants, saviour siblings **178**.28-31
stem cells **144**.15, 17-18
from bone marrow **144**.21, 23
stepfamilies **124**.23-8, 39
benefits **124**.25
children's worries **124**.23, 26
parents' worries **124**.27-8
statistics **124**.23, 24, 25
step-parenting **124**.39
sterile-seed (Terminator) technology **138**.18
sterilisation and fertility **178**.4
steroids *see* anabolic agents/steroids
STIs *see* sexually transmitted infections
stimulants (uppers) **118**.36-7; **163**.2, 4-5
see also amphetamines; cocaine; ecstasy
stop and search **128**.35; **147**.35-7; **177**.34
stopping cannabis use **128**.2, 10
stopping smoking *see* smoking, giving up
store cards **134**.22; **180**.14, 26
and personal data **168**.8
storms, and climate change **151**.8
street children **99**.1, 18-19
as tourist sights **156**.33-4
street crime **177**.4-5
street drinking **130**.12
street fighting **177**.5
street homelessness **130**.9-12
numbers **130**.9-10
reasons for **130**.10-11
street lifestyles **130**.12
stress **107**.8, 18

Volume numbers appear first (in bold) followed by page numbers; a change in volume number is preceded by a semi-colon.

Vol. 76 The Water Crisis
Vol. 78 Threatened Species
Vol. 81 Alternative Therapies
Vol. 88 Food and Nutrition
Vol. 89 Refugees
Vol. 97 Energy Matters
Vol. 99 Exploited Children
Vol. 100 Stress and Anxiety
Vol. 107 Work Issues
Vol. 116 Grief and Loss
Vol. 118 Focus on Sport
Vol. 119 Transport Trends
Vol. 121 The Censorship Debate
Vol. 124 Parenting Issues
Vol. 125 Understanding Depression
Vol. 127 Eating Disorders
Vol. 128 The Cannabis Issue
Vol. 129 Gambling Trends
Vol. 130 Homelessness
Vol. 133 Teen Pregnancy and Lone Parents
Vol. 134 Customers and Consumerism
Vol. 135 Coping with Disability
Vol. 136 Self-Harm

Vol. 138 A Genetically Modified Future?
Vol. 139 The Education Problem
Vol. 140 Vegetarian and Vegan Diets
Vol. 141 Mental Health
Vol. 142 Media Issues
Vol. 143 Problem Drinking
Vol. 144 The Cloning Debate
Vol. 145 Smoking Trends
Vol. 146 Sustainability and Environment
Vol. 147 The Terrorism Problem
Vol. 148 Religious Beliefs
Vol. 149 A Classless Society?
Vol. 150 Migration and Population
Vol. 151 Climate Change
Vol. 152 Euthanasia and the Right to Die
Vol. 153 Sexual Orientation and Society
Vol. 154 The Gender Gap
Vol. 155 Domestic Abuse
Vol. 156 Travel and Tourism
Vol. 157 The Problem of Globalisation
Vol. 158 The Internet Revolution
Vol. 159 An Ageing Population
Vol. 160 Poverty and Exclusion

Vol. 161 Waste Issues
Vol. 162 Staying Fit
Vol. 163 Drugs in the UK
Vol. 164 The AIDS Crisis
Vol. 165 Bullying Issues
Vol. 166 Marriage and Cohabitation
Vol. 167 Our Human Rights
Vol. 168 Privacy and Surveillance
Vol. 169 The Animal Rights Debate
Vol. 170 Body Image and Self-Esteem
Vol. 171 Abortion – Rights and Ethics
Vol. 172 Racial and Ethnic Discrimination
Vol. 173 Sexual Health
Vol. 174 Selling Sex
Vol. 175 Citizenship and Participation
Vol. 176 Health Issues for Young People
Vol. 177 Crime in the UK
Vol. 178 Reproductive Ethics
Vol. 179 Tackling Child Abuse
Vol. 180 Money and Finances
Vol. 181 The Housing Issue

avoiding **141**.36
and anxiety **100**.2, 21
coping with **100**.27-39
defining **100**.1, 5, 33
and eating disorders **127**.16
and exams **176**.5, 38-9
and exercise **141**.39; **162**.37
factors determining degree of **100**.14-15
and fertility **178**.5
'fight or flight' response to **100**.1, 14-15, 25, 28
harmful effects of **100**.28, 38
health benefits of the right sort of **100**.39
in laboratory animals **169**.16, 21
and lifestyle **100**.19, 31-2
positive and negative **100**.14
school stress **176**.37, 38-9
signs and symptoms of **100**.1, 2, 5, 12, 28-9, 33, 35
statistics on **100**.13, 19
at work **165**.34
stress management **100**.32, 36
strokes **159**.4
and depression **125**.5
stem cell therapy **144**.22
structural adjustment **157**.7
students **107**.33, 35-6
accommodation **181**.18, 19-20
applying to university **139**.29-32
and parental educational level **149**.7, 31, 35
health issues **176**.5-6
living at home **149**.2
and money matters **134**.24; **139**.34-5; **180**.28-9, 32-3
budgeting **180**.30-31
costs of a university education **139**.34, 35
graduate starting salaries **139**.35, 36
grants **180**.28, 33
income and expenditure **180**.32-3
loans **139**.34; **180**.28, 33
part-time work **139**.35
from overseas, entry allowed **150**.23
statistics **139**.2, 32
and terrorism **147**.13-14
substance abuse
and homelessness **130**.11, 20
see also alcohol; drug abuse; solvent abuse
suction aspiration (abortion) **171**.2
suffering, animals
and animal experiments **169**.14-15, 16, 25
animal transport **169**.10
emotional **169**.2
fur farming **169**.5
intensively farmed chickens **169**.13
suicidal feelings
after bereavement **116**.4
and bullying **165**.20, 21-2
children **176**.35, 36-7
suicide **136**.27-39
bereavement by **116**.8
and depression **125**.10, 22
impact on others **136**.28
and the Internet **136**.37-9
and the media **136**.37; **142**.30

men **125**.15
prevention
how to help **136**.29
initiatives **136**.31, 32, 36
reasons for **136**.27
risk factors for **136**.25-6, 27, 30
and self-harm **136**.2, 9, 11, 24-6
statistics **125**.16; **136**.31, 33, 34, 35
suicide pacts and the Internet **136**.39
support for suicidal people **136**.27-8
Samaritans **136**.29, 32, 37
warning signs of **136**.11, 29, 30
see also assisted suicide; attempted suicide; physician-assisted suicide (PAS)
sulphur dioxide (SO2) emissions **119**.15; **146**.35
sunbeds and cancer **176**.10-11
supercasinos **129**.14-16, 34
supermarkets
and Fairtrade **134**.36
and free-range eggs **140**.38
and GM products **138**.26
impact on communities **134**.38
packaging waste **161**.12
and plastic bags **161**.13-14
and vegetarianism **140**.20
supervision orders **177**.17, 26
supplements **118**.35
and anti-doping rules **118**.33
nutritional **118**.28
support groups
alcohol abuse **143**.38, 39
domestic abuse perpetrators **155**.33-4
domestic abuse sufferers **155**.6-7, 28-9
gamblers **129**.37
self-harmers **136**.3, 21
sexual abusers **179**.22-3
surgery, weight loss **162**.3
surgical abortion **171**.2
surrogacy **178**.7-8, 13-14
surveillance **147**.29
by the government **168**.4-5, 7-8, 13-14, 27, 35
and law **168**.10-11
by local authorities **168**.20-21
online **168**.32-3
risks **168**.4
by satellite **168**.26-7
suspended sentence orders **177**.26
sustainability **146**.1-11
construction industry **146**.11
consumption **146**.7, 8
definition **146**.3
fossil fuels **151**.28-30
Millennium Development Goals **160**.32
production **146**.7, 8
seafood **146**.29
UK principles **146**.3
UK strategy **146**.8-9
sustainable agriculture **88**.32-3; **146**.27
sustainable communities **146**.9
sustainable development
and global water supplies **76**.17, 31

sustainable housing 181.39
sustainable population 150.31-2
sustainable tourism 156.8, 22-3, 24
   attitudes to 156.29-30
sustainable use of space 146.17
swearing on television 121.38-9
sweatshops 157.27-9

T

t-GURTS 138.18
tabloid newspapers 142.8
tactile warning devices, cars 119.19
tagging of asylum seekers 89.36-7
tai chi 81.3, 14, 30, 31, 39
talking therapies 125.29-30; 141.35
   access to 125.30-31
tariffs see trade barriers
Tasers 177.31-2
taxation 180.24
   on aviation fuel 119.16
   carbon tax on fuel 97.25
   Child Tax Credit (CTC) 133.33
     overpayments to lone-parent families 124.35; 133.30
   and civil partnerships 153.28
   congestion tax 119.34
   contributions 89.23, 30
   fraud and error 133.36
   fuel taxes 119.14, 24
   gambling 129.18
   and income inequality 160.6
   landfill tax 161.12, 20, 35
   on savings interest 180.26
   tobacco 145.17
   and trade 157.12-13
   Working Tax Credit 133.35
tea, fairtrade 157.33-4
teachers
   concerns about CCTV in schools 168.25
   gender gap 154.25
   homophobic bullying 153.14, 16, 17

numbers of 139.1, 12
   salaries 139.12
   and stress in young people 100.1
   and workplace stress 100.12
team sports participation 118.4
technological change, and workplace stress 100.16
teenage fathers 133.25-7
teenage magazines 142.28
teenage mothers 133.18-24
   education 133.24
   public attitudes to 133.18, 21
   single mothers 133.28
teenage parenthood, long-term effects 133.10
teenage parents 133.20-27
   see also teenage fathers; teenage mothers
teenage pregnancies 176.4
   and abortion 133.9
   and adoption 133.8-9
   advice 133.8
   as biologically natural 133.19
   keeping the baby 133.8
   options 133.8-9
   planned 133.20
   and poverty 133.20
   statistics 133.2, 4, 5-6, 12, 17
telecommunications, broadband 158.5-6
telephones
  communications database 168.13-14
   mobile see mobile phones
   telephone sales and consumer rights 134.20
television 158.5
   advertising and children 134.10, 12
   alcohol advertising 143.19, 20
   children's viewing 121.27
     control of 158.32
   and disabled people 135.29, 32, 35
   and homosexuality 153.23-5
   influence on young people 145.6
   as news source 142.33
   offensive language 121.38-9
   online 158.21-2
   reality television, promoting racial understanding 115.22

Volume numbers appear first (in bold) followed by page numbers; a change in volume number is preceded by a semi-colon.

Vol. 76 The Water Crisis
Vol. 78 Threatened Species
Vol. 81 Alternative Therapies
Vol. 88 Food and Nutrition
Vol. 89 Refugees
Vol. 97 Energy Matters
Vol. 99 Exploited Children
Vol. 100 Stress and Anxiety
Vol. 107 Work Issues
Vol. 116 Grief and Loss
Vol. 118 Focus on Sport
Vol. 119 Transport Trends
Vol. 121 The Censorship Debate
Vol. 124 Parenting Issues
Vol. 125 Understanding Depression
Vol. 127 Eating Disorders
Vol. 128 The Cannabis Issue
Vol. 129 Gambling Trends
Vol. 130 Homelessness
Vol. 133 Teen Pregnancy and Lone Parents
Vol. 134 Customers and Consumerism
Vol. 135 Coping with Disability
Vol. 136 Self-Harm

Vol. 138 A Genetically Modified Future?
Vol. 139 The Education Problem
Vol. 140 Vegetarian and Vegan Diets
Vol. 141 Mental Health
Vol. 142 Media Issues
Vol. 143 Problem Drinking
Vol. 144 The Cloning Debate
Vol. 145 Smoking Trends
Vol. 146 Sustainability and Environment
Vol. 147 The Terrorism Problem
Vol. 148 Religious Beliefs
Vol. 149 A Classless Society?
Vol. 150 Migration and Population
Vol. 151 Climate Change
Vol. 152 Euthanasia and the Right to Die
Vol. 153 Sexual Orientation and Society
Vol. 154 The Gender Gap
Vol. 155 Domestic Abuse
Vol. 156 Travel and Tourism
Vol. 157 The Problem of Globalisation
Vol. 158 The Internet Revolution
Vol. 159 An Ageing Population
Vol. 160 Poverty and Exclusion

Vol. 161 Waste Issues
Vol. 162 Staying Fit
Vol. 163 Drugs in the UK
Vol. 164 The AIDS Crisis
Vol. 165 Bullying Issues
Vol. 166 Marriage and Cohabitation
Vol. 167 Our Human Rights
Vol. 168 Privacy and Surveillance
Vol. 169 The Animal Rights Debate
Vol. 170 Body Image and Self-Esteem
Vol. 171 Abortion – Rights and Ethics
Vol. 172 Racial and Ethnic Discrimination
Vol. 173 Sexual Health
Vol. 174 Selling Sex
Vol. 175 Citizenship and Participation
Vol. 176 Health Issues for Young People
Vol. 177 Crime in the UK
Vol. 178 Reproductive Ethics
Vol. 179 Tackling Child Abuse
Vol. 180 Money and Finances
Vol. 181 The Housing Issue

regulation 121.36-7
soaps
    and offensive language 121.38
    and teenage drinking 143.18-19
watershed 121.37, 38-9
and women's sport 118.21
young people's viewing habits 142.38
telomeres and ageing 159.32, 33; 162.12
temporary accommodation 130.9
numbers of households 130.5, 13-14
and older people 130.18
tenancy support services 130.29
tenants
council tenants' rights to move 181.35-6
rights 181.16
terminally ill people
assisted suicide see assisted suicide
euthanasia see euthanasia
Terminator (sterile-seed) technology 138.18
terms of trade 157.7
territorial privacy 168.2
terrorism 147.1-25
countering 147.26-39
definition 147.1, 4
fear of 147.12
history 147.1, 4-5
and identity cards 131.14; 168.16, 18
and the Internet 147.8-9
and Islamophobia 131.11
London bombings 115.27, 36
public support for anti-terrorism measures 167.24
reaction to 147.10-11, 38-9
and satellite surveillance 168.27
statistics 147.6
targeting terrorist funds 147.3, 28-9
Terrorism Acts 147.3, 27, 35-6
timeline 147.5
effect on tourism 156.8
types 147.1
text messages
bullying 165.23
preventing unwanted texts 134.28
THC (delta-9 tetrahydrocannabinol)
and cannabis strength 128.3
effect on brain 128.34
therapeutic cloning 144.2, 15, 16, 26; 178.34
embryonic stem cells 144.25
humanist view of 144.7; 178.36-7
therapeutic exemption forms 118.31-2
tidal energy 97.2, 6, 12
timber production 146.30-31
timber recycling 161.25
time limit for abortion 171.29, 30, 31, 32-4
time management, and stress 100.27, 29, 32, 36
tins, recycling 161.27
tiredness and bereavement 116.19
TNCs see transnational corporations
tobacco
advertising ban 145.7
chemical contents of smoke 145.1
consumption 145.4, 22

deaths 163.11
and the economy 145.22-3
and pharming of HIV drugs 138.21-2
plants 145.25
production 145.22-3
see also smoking
tobacco industry
control of 145.23, 24
effect of smoking ban 145.16-17
tofu 140.6, 20
toilets, lack of in developing countries 146.14-15
tolerance
to alcohol 143.7
to drugs 163.2
TOMPS (toxic organic micropollutants) 146.35-6
tools, recycling 161.25
torture 167.25-7
evidence obtained under torture 167.27
victims 89.18-20
touch screen software 158.22-3
tour operators 156.1, 8-9
tourism
best and worst sights 156.6
and bullfighting 169.38
child sex tourism 99.17, 20, 23, 25-6; 156.37-9
and climate change 156.1, 25, 28-30
dependency on 156.21
effects of 156.20-39
environmental impact 156.20, 21, 22, 25
gap years 156.15-19
industry 156.8-9
Internet bookings 156.1, 13, 14
statistics 156.3-4, 7, 10
trends 156.1-14
visits to the UK 156.3-4, 10, 13
see also ecotourism; responsible tourism
tourists
behaviour 156.31
unconcerned about environmental impact 156.28-30
visiting threatened environments 156.27
tower blocks and racial segregation 115.32
toxic chemicals
and water pollution 76.11
toxic organic micropollutants (TOMPS) 146.35-6
trade, international see international trade
trade in endangered species 78.16-17, 19-22; 146.34
and traditional medicine 78.23
and the UK 78.38-9
trade liberalisation 157.12, 20
see also free trade
trade rules 157.17
fairness 157.17-18, 25
trade unions 107.31
and workplace stress 100.11, 26
trading standards 88.38-9
traffic see road traffic
traffic pollution see pollution and transport
trafficking 167.20, 21, 22
children 99.1, 3, 4; 167.32, 34
EU laws 179.29
and the sexual exploitation of children 99.3, 16, 17, 20,

21, 24, 28
    women **150**.15
training
    and age discrimination **159**.9
    disabled people **135**.15
    opportunities, racial discrimination **115**.14
    and starting a business **107**.4, 34
    and workplace stress **100**.16
trains *see* railways
transgender people **153**.13
    and equality **154**.4
transgenic bacteria **144**.11
transnational corporations (TNCs) **157**.7
    and the environment **157**.10-11
    see also multinational corporations
transport
    census information **150**.36
    and climate change reduction **151**.39
    and disabled people **135**.7-9
    emissions *see* emissions, transport
    and energy efficiency **97**.24, 25, 31
    environmental **134**.30, 32
    live animals **169**.10
    public attitudes to **97**.35, 36
    spending on **134**.4, 25
    trends **119**.1-16, 29-31; **161**.31-2
transsexualism **149**.5; **153**.13
transvestism **153**.13
trapping for fur **169**.5, 8
traumatic bereavements **116**.10-12
travel
    documents **89**.33, 35
    ethical **134**.30
    and terrorism **147**.32
travel agents **156**.9
travellers' cheques **180**.13-14
Travellers of Irish Heritage, and education **115**.18
treatment
    alcohol abuse **143**.35, 38-9
    depression **125**.24-39
    eating disorders **127**.28-9
        binge eating **127**.16

    bulimia **127**.14
    manic depression **125**.19-20
    obesity **127**.34; **162**.2-3, 6, 20
    post-natal depression **125**.17-18
    Seasonal Affective Disorder **125**.18
    self-harm **136**.11
trees
    planting and carbon offsetting **151**.35
    planting as way of remembrance **116**.17
tricyclics **125**.32
troposphere warming **151**.4
truancy rates **139**.2
tuberculosis and HIV **164**.30
twins, IVF, and health problems **178**.21-2
two-earner families **149**.28

U

U film classification **121**.29
UK
    and children's rights **167**.38
    domestic tourisn **156**.10
    drugs policy criticized **128**.38
    ecological debt **146**.4-6
    economy
        benefits from globalisation **157**.1
    competition from overseas **157**.35-6
    genetically modified crops **138**.2-3, 5, 39
    Human Rights Act **167**.3, 4, 5, 15-18
    income inequality **160**.6, 7
    natural environment conservation **146**.32-3
    online gambling market **129**.19, 20
    population, ethnic groups **115**.3
    poverty **160**.1-24
    and sustainable development **146**.3, 8-9
    supercasino **129**.14-16
    tourism industry **156**.7-10, 13
    tourist sights **156**.6
    travel abroad **156**.1, 4
umbilical cord
    blood storage **178**.33

Volume numbers appear first (in bold) followed by page numbers; a change in volume number is preceded by a semi-colon.

Vol. 76 The Water Crisis
Vol. 78 Threatened Species
Vol. 81 Alternative Therapies
Vol. 88 Food and Nutrition
Vol. 89 Refugees
Vol. 97 Energy Matters
Vol. 99 Exploited Children
Vol. 100 Stress and Anxiety
Vol. 107 Work Issues
Vol. 116 Grief and Loss
Vol. 118 Focus on Sport
Vol. 119 Transport Trends
Vol. 121 The Censorship Debate
Vol. 124 Parenting Issues
Vol. 125 Understanding Depression
Vol. 127 Eating Disorders
Vol. 128 The Cannabis Issue
Vol. 129 Gambling Trends
Vol. 130 Homelessness
Vol. 133 Teen Pregnancy and Lone Parents
Vol. 134 Customers and Consumerism
Vol. 135 Coping with Disability
Vol. 136 Self-Harm

Vol. 138 A Genetically Modified Future?
Vol. 139 The Education Problem
Vol. 140 Vegetarian and Vegan Diets
Vol. 141 Mental Health
Vol. 142 Media Issues
Vol. 143 Problem Drinking
Vol. 144 The Cloning Debate
Vol. 145 Smoking Trends
Vol. 146 Sustainability and Environment
Vol. 147 The Terrorism Problem
Vol. 148 Religious Beliefs
Vol. 149 A Classless Society?
Vol. 150 Migration and Population
Vol. 151 Climate Change
Vol. 152 Euthanasia and the Right to Die
Vol. 153 Sexual Orientation and Society
Vol. 154 The Gender Gap
Vol. 155 Domestic Abuse
Vol. 156 Travel and Tourism
Vol. 157 The Problem of Globalisation
Vol. 158 The Internet Revolution
Vol. 159 An Ageing Population
Vol. 160 Poverty and Exclusion

Vol. 161 Waste Issues
Vol. 162 Staying Fit
Vol. 163 Drugs in the UK
Vol. 164 The AIDS Crisis
Vol. 165 Bullying Issues
Vol. 166 Marriage and Cohabitation
Vol. 167 Our Human Rights
Vol. 168 Privacy and Surveillance
Vol. 169 The Animal Rights Debate
Vol. 170 Body Image and Self-Esteem
Vol. 171 Abortion – Rights and Ethics
Vol. 172 Racial and Ethnic Discrimination
Vol. 173 Sexual Health
Vol. 174 Selling Sex
Vol. 175 Citizenship and Participation
Vol. 176 Health Issues for Young People
Vol. 177 Crime in the UK
Vol. 178 Reproductive Ethics
Vol. 179 Tackling Child Abuse
Vol. 180 Money and Finances
Vol. 181 The Housing Issue

stem cells 178.28
UN see United Nations
unauthorized absence (truancy) 139.2
underachievement, black pupils 115.19-21
underage drinking 176.17-18
    and depression 125.9
    ideas for reducing 143.5, 29
    underage purchase of alcohol 143.16, 20, 28
    see also young people and alcohol
underage gambling 129.1
    National Lottery 129.11-13
    online gambling 129.18, 25
    online poker 129.25
underage purchase of tobacco 145.3
underground travel and disabled people 135.9
unemployment 107.10, 37-9
    and adult children living with parents 181.4
    and depression, men 125.14-15
    disabled people 135.3
    and incapacity benefit 100.23
    jobseekers allowance (JSA) 100.23
    and migration 150.9-10
    and poverty 160.2
    and social housing 181.35
    young people 149.38-9
UNICEF, Convention on the Rights of the Child 167.28-9
union jack 131.3-4
unions 107.31
unipolar (endogenous) depression 125.4, 10
United Nations (UN) 157.8
    and HIV/AIDS 164.32, 39
    human rights treaties 167.1
    UN Committee on the Rights of the Child, and corporal
        punishment 167.36; 179.30, 31
    UN Convention on the Rights of the Child 167.28-9
    UN Conventions on drugs 128.26
units of alcohol 143.1, 26; 176.15
    awareness of 143.11
    drink labelling 143.30, 32
Universal Declaration of Human Rights 76.24; 89.6; 167.8-
    10, 14
    and privacy 168.3
universal social pension 159.24
universities
    admissions and exam stress 100.7
    application numbers 139.31, 32
    costs of a university education 139.34, 35
    courses 139.2, 29, 30, 38-9
    discrimination against middle-class applications 149.7
    'dumbing down' accusations 149.7
    fees 139.34
    and integration 115.30
    post-qualification admission 139.16
    school background of students 149.34-5
    selection and parental education 149.7, 31, 35
    and social class 149.1-2
    student finance 180.28-9, 32-3
    see also degrees; further education; students
unmarried parents 124.22
upbringing and gender development 154.1
urban areas and climate change 151.10-12

urban growth 146.17, 24
urbanization 150.33, 35, 37-8
utilitarian drug use 163.1

V

v-GURTs 138.18
vaccination
    and organic farming 140.35-6
    search for AIDS vaccine 164.34-6
vaccine damage compensation 135.5
vacuum aspiration (abortion) 171.2
value for money, and consumer rights 134.2
values
    and Britishness 131.1
    human 148.15
    religious 148.16
vascular dementia 141.6
vascular diseases and depression 125.5
veganism 140.2, 7, 25-6
    costs of 140.25
    and health 140.25
    and protein 140.23-4
    and restaurants 140.25
vegetarian diets 140.2, 6, 7
vegetarianism 88.18; 140.1-26
    definition 140.1, 5
    eating out 140.5, 25
    and food ingredients 140.18
    number of vegetarians 140.20, 39
    reasons for becoming vegetarian 140.1, 5, 8, 14
    and supermarkets 140.20
vehicles
    adaptations for diability 135.7
    recycling 161.23
verbal abuse
    of children with learning difficulties 165.15
    homophobic 165.13
    shouting at children 179.39
victimization 153.38
    and racism 115.7-8
        at work 115.11-12
victims of abuse
    blamed for abuse 155.2, 3
    male 155.12-13
    reasons for not leaving 155.5, 6, 7
    reluctance to speak out 155.3-4, 30-31
    support for 155.6-7, 28-9
victims of bullying
    experiences 165.2, 5, 10, 14, 15, 16, 17
    helping 165.6, 7-8
victims of crime
    racial identity 115.10
    victim-offender mediation 177.31
video games
    and body image 170.27
    and children 121.32-3
video sharing sites 142.35
videos
    abusive 165.31

and children **121**.26
onine **158**.21-2
regulation **121**.26, 31
see also films
violence
against girls **154**.13-14
against children **167**.36-9
and computer games **121**.33, 35; **158**.33
disabled people as victims **135**.27
and male depression **125**.15
in the media **121**.34
effect on children **121**.28, 33, 34, 35
and young people **176**.4
see also corporal punishment; domestic abuse; physical abuse
violent street crime **177**.4-5
violent extremism **147**.33-4
vitamins **140**.4
in meat **140**.12
and teenage diet **176**.8-9
vitrification of embryos **178**.22
vocational degree subjects **139**.38-9
vocational qualifications **139**.4, 18
gender difference **139**.10
see also specialist diplomas
vocational training and age discrimination **159**.9
volatile substance abuse *see* solvent abuse
voluntary activity, England **131**.3
gap years **156**.15-19
voluntary euthanasia *see* assisted suicide
voting **131**.16, 17, 18
eligibility to vote **131**.16, 18, 30
lowering voting age **131**.28, 29, 30
reasons for not voting **131**.22
voter apathy **131**.22
voter turnout **131**.19-21
vulnerable people, effect of legalizing euthanasia **152**.6-7

W

wages
and child domestic workers **99**.9, 10

footballers **118**.11
effect of immigration **150**.17
migrant workers **150**.9
minimum wage **107**.31
multinational companies **157**.11
see also earnings; incomes; salaries
waist measurement and exercise **162**.36
walking
as alternative to car **119**.25
health benefits of **119**.27
to school **119**.25, 26, 27
see also exercise; pedestrians
war
effect on disabled people **135**.26
on terror **89**.8; **167**.22-3
war-affected children **99**.32-5
and the effects of armed conflict **99**.33
help for **99**.34
problem of **99**.32
testimonials of **99**.33-4
warranties, consumer rights **134**.18-19
waste
amounts **161**.1, 3-5, 22
as animal food **140**.17
collection **161**.6
construction industry **146**.11
definition **161**.1
and energy generation **97**.37, 39; **161**.20, 38, 39
food **161**.4, 10-11, 19
government strategy **161**.20
hazardous **161**.1, 6, 32
incineration **161**.7
reducing waste **161**.18, 19, 20, 38
sorting **161**.25
and water consumption **76**.1, 4, 19, 32, 36
water companies **88**.31
contact with schools **76**.1
multinational water corporations **76**.22, 23, 29-30
responsibilities of **76**.1
and water bills in the UK **76**.33
and water conservation **76**.36
water conservation **76**.1, 3, 22, 37-9

Volume numbers appear first (in bold) followed by page numbers; a change in volume number is preceded by a semi-colon.

Vol. 76 The Water Crisis
Vol. 78 Threatened Species
Vol. 81 Alternative Therapies
Vol. 88 Food and Nutrition
Vol. 89 Refugees
Vol. 97 Energy Matters
Vol. 99 Exploited Children
Vol. 100 Stress and Anxiety
Vol. 107 Work Issues
Vol. 116 Grief and Loss
Vol. 118 Focus on Sport
Vol. 119 Transport Trends
Vol. 121 The Censorship Debate
Vol. 124 Parenting Issues
Vol. 125 Understanding Depression
Vol. 127 Eating Disorders
Vol. 128 The Cannabis Issue
Vol. 129 Gambling Trends
Vol. 130 Homelessness
Vol. 133 Teen Pregnancy and Lone Parents
Vol. 134 Customers and Consumerism
Vol. 135 Coping with Disability
Vol. 136 Self-Harm

Vol. 138 A Genetically Modified Future?
Vol. 139 The Education Problem
Vol. 140 Vegetarian and Vegan Diets
Vol. 141 Mental Health
Vol. 142 Media Issues
Vol. 143 Problem Drinking
Vol. 144 The Cloning Debate
Vol. 145 Smoking Trends
Vol. 146 Sustainability and Environment
Vol. 147 The Terrorism Problem
Vol. 148 Religious Beliefs
Vol. 149 A Classless Society?
Vol. 150 Migration and Population
Vol. 151 Climate Change
Vol. 152 Euthanasia and the Right to Die
Vol. 153 Sexual Orientation and Society
Vol. 154 The Gender Gap
Vol. 155 Domestic Abuse
Vol. 156 Travel and Tourism
Vol. 157 The Problem of Globalisation
Vol. 158 The Internet Revolution
Vol. 159 An Ageing Population
Vol. 160 Poverty and Exclusion

Vol. 161 Waste Issues
Vol. 162 Staying Fit
Vol. 163 Drugs in the UK
Vol. 164 The AIDS Crisis
Vol. 165 Bullying Issues
Vol. 166 Marriage and Cohabitation
Vol. 167 Our Human Rights
Vol. 168 Privacy and Surveillance
Vol. 169 The Animal Rights Debate
Vol. 170 Body Image and Self-Esteem
Vol. 171 Abortion – Rights and Ethics
Vol. 172 Racial and Ethnic Discrimination
Vol. 173 Sexual Health
Vol. 174 Selling Sex
Vol. 175 Citizenship and Participation
Vol. 176 Health Issues for Young People
Vol. 177 Crime in the UK
Vol. 178 Reproductive Ethics
Vol. 179 Tackling Child Abuse
Vol. 180 Money and Finances
Vol. 181 The Housing Issue

answering questions about 76.36
in everyday life 76.27
in the garden 76.1, 36, 37, 38
in the home 76.37, 38
investment in 76.27
in schools 76.39
and showers 76.1, 27, 37, 38
and toilet flushing 76.2, 27, 37, 38
water consumption
bottled water 76.23, 27
clean water as measure of poverty 160.28
and eco-systems 76.2, 16-17, 19
groundwater sources for drinking 76.7, 9, 12
and the importance of water quality 76.9
lack of access to clean water 76.8, 9
largest users of water 76.36
and population growth 76.22, 29
reasons for growth in 76.3, 5, 8
in selected countries 76.7
statistics 76.7, 9
and waste 76.1, 4, 19, 32, 36
water requirements per person per day 76.6
and water shortages 76.21-2
water cycle 76.2, 21
water filters, recycling 161.25
water management
and agriculture 76.18
costs of 76.33
dealing with the water crisis 76.22, 26-8
government and planned policies of 76.8-9, 17
and multinational water corporations 76.29-30
pricing mechanisms 76.22, 32
and privatisation 76.22-3, 32
and wars over the ownership of water resources 76.22
water meters 76.36, 38
water pollution 76.1, 5, 10-11; 146.36
causes of 76.4, 7, 8, 9
in the developed world 76.10-11
in developing countries 76.4, 10
and global water supplies 76.10-11, 15
and multinational water corporations 76.29-30
statistics 76.9
and water shortages 76.36
water stress, calculating 76.15-16, 17
water supplies 76.15-17
financing the provision of 76.31-2
and food production 76.3, 4, 7, 18
and multinational water corporations 76.29-30
and planned water management policies 76.8-9, 17
projected worldwide water use 76.35
statistics 76.1, 2, 4, 6, 8, 19, 20
and water as a human right 76.24-5, 32
and water pollution 76.10-11, 15; 146.36
and water shortages 76.15-17, 19, 21-2; 146.13
water usage by sector 76.3
and water users 76.36
watershed, television 121.37
erosion of 121.38-9
wave power 97.2, 6, 12
wealth
children's perceptions of 149.9-12

inequality 149.19, 22, 27
and segregation 115.32
weapons
and crime 177.15-16, 29-30
and the law 177.7, 30
and sentences 177.38-9
young people's concerns 177.15-16
Web 2.0 158.6
websites
and bullying 165.24
and child sexual abuse 179.17
selling repossessed properties 181.7
and suicide 136.37-9
terrorist 147.8-9
weight see body weight; obesity
weight loss
drug treatment 162.2-3, 6, 20
and exercise 162.20, 36
financial incentives 162.22-3
and lifestyle changes 162.20
surgery 162.3
weight management 127.34; 176.7
weight monitoring in schools 127.36; 162.16
well-being, teaching 170.14-15
whales
hunting 78.6, 13, 14
watching 78.13-14
wild animals
as food 140.17
and the fur trade 169.5, 6, 8
wildlife
captive breeding 78.22
conservation 88.32, 34; 146.33
and the exotic pet trade 78.21-2
crime 78.19, 38-9
illegal souvenirs 156.32
illegal trade in 78.21-2
killing of 78.2, 4-5, 5-6
and the law 78.16-17, 38-9
overcollecting 78.22
rare species 78.28
trade 146.34
live animals 78.20-1
vulnerable species 78.28
and water abstraction 76.34, 36
see also conservation; endangered species; extinction
wills, lone parents 133.38
wind energy 97.2, 4, 5, 6, 9, 21, 38
and climate change 97.15
costs of 97.16
energy available from 97.5
new wind farm projects 97.5
and noise 97.17
numbers of wind farms 97.11
offshore 97.12, 16, 26
opposition to wind farms 97.12
public attitudes to 97.16
top myths about 97.15-17
turbines 97.5, 15, 17, 38
in the UK 97.13, 26
withdrawal symptoms

cannabis **128**.15
gambling **129**.30
nicotine **145**.26-7
withdrawing or withholding treatment **152**.3, 5-6
womb damage and fertility **178**.4
women
  and abortion
    abortion to save mother's life **171**.22
    right to choose **171**.28
    right to life **171**.17
    views on abortion time limit **171**.29
  and ageing population **159**.5
  and alcohol
    and heart attack risk **143**.7
    increasing consumption **176**.14
    pregnant women **143**.3, 25, 27, 33-4
  and body image *see* body image, women
  credit card usage, global **180**.19
  disabled, violence against **135**.27
  employment prospects **107**.32
  equality and child labour **99**.12
  and fertility *see* fertility
  and financial independence **180**.17-18
  and the future of work **107**.12
  and gambling **129**.21, 34
    online gambling **129**.27
  gender pay gap **107**.13, 25, 26; **154**.2-3, 6, 30, 35-9
  glass cliff/glass ceiling **107**.9; **154**.34, 38
  and globalisation **157**.4
  graduate salaries **139**.36
  and HIV/AIDS **96**.20, 24-5, 29, 30-1; **164**.5-6
    in pregnancy **164**.3, 25, 27, 29-30, 31
  and homelessness **130**.15
  and household finance roles **180**.18-19
  Internet usage **158**.4
  low self-esteem **136**.2
  marriage expectations **166**.3
  marriage risks **166**.11
  maternity leave **107**.16, 21
  and mental ill-health **141**.1
  and migration **150**.2, 15
  older women and IVF **178**.17, 19-20

and online shopping **134**.16
and part-time working **107**.17
post-natal depression **125**.4, 17-18
and poverty **160**.15, 25
pregnant women **88**.7
and sexually transmitted infections (STIs) **96**.3, 9
size zero aspirations **170**.20
and smoking **145**.21, 22
social mobility **149**.21
sperm creation **144**.29
in sport **118**.18-20, 21-2
and stress **100**.13
  frequent worrying **100**.19
and suicide **136**.33, 35
working mothers **107**.26
women in the workforce **149**.21; **154**.29-34
  equal pay *see* gender pay gap
  European Union **154**.33
  glass ceiling **107**.9; **154**.38
  glass cliff **107**.9; **154**.34
  in the media **154**.11
  non-traditional careers **154**.31-2
  in senior positions **154**.17, 29, 34
  see also working mothers
work
  effects of cannabis use **128**.14
  gambling at work **129**.22-4
  and mobile phones **158**.13
  past retirement age **159**.10, 15
  see also child labour; employment; migrant workers; slavery
work experience and specialist diplomas **139**.24, 25
work-life balance **107**.6, 14, 16; **154**.30
  see also hours of work
working abroad **107**.3
working class **149**.3
  attitudes to money **149**.19-20
  attitudes to moving home **149**.26
working conditions
  garment industry **157**.27-9
  international companies **157**.11
  migrants **150**.19, 20
working hours *see* hours of work

Volume numbers appear first (in bold) followed by page numbers; a change in volume number is preceded by a semi-colon.

Vol. 76 The Water Crisis
Vol. 78 Threatened Species
Vol. 81 Alternative Therapies
Vol. 88 Food and Nutrition
Vol. 89 Refugees
Vol. 97 Energy Matters
Vol. 99 Exploited Children
Vol. 100 Stress and Anxiety
Vol. 107 Work Issues
Vol. 116 Grief and Loss
Vol. 118 Focus on Sport
Vol. 119 Transport Trends
Vol. 121 The Censorship Debate
Vol. 124 Parenting Issues
Vol. 125 Understanding Depression
Vol. 127 Eating Disorders
Vol. 128 The Cannabis Issue
Vol. 129 Gambling Trends
Vol. 130 Homelessness
Vol. 133 Teen Pregnancy and Lone Parents
Vol. 134 Customers and Consumerism
Vol. 135 Coping with Disability
Vol. 136 Self-Harm

Vol. 138 A Genetically Modified Future?
Vol. 139 The Education Problem
Vol. 140 Vegetarian and Vegan Diets
Vol. 141 Mental Health
Vol. 142 Media Issues
Vol. 143 Problem Drinking
Vol. 144 The Cloning Debate
Vol. 145 Smoking Trends
Vol. 146 Sustainability and Environment
Vol. 147 The Terrorism Problem
Vol. 148 Religious Beliefs
Vol. 149 A Classless Society?
Vol. 150 Migration and Population
Vol. 151 Climate Change
Vol. 152 Euthanasia and the Right to Die
Vol. 153 Sexual Orientation and Society
Vol. 154 The Gender Gap
Vol. 155 Domestic Abuse
Vol. 156 Travel and Tourism
Vol. 157 The Problem of Globalisation
Vol. 158 The Internet Revolution
Vol. 159 An Ageing Population
Vol. 160 Poverty and Exclusion

Vol. 161 Waste Issues
Vol. 162 Staying Fit
Vol. 163 Drugs in the UK
Vol. 164 The AIDS Crisis
Vol. 165 Bullying Issues
Vol. 166 Marriage and Cohabitation
Vol. 167 Our Human Rights
Vol. 168 Privacy and Surveillance
Vol. 169 The Animal Rights Debate
Vol. 170 Body Image and Self-Esteem
Vol. 171 Abortion – Rights and Ethics
Vol. 172 Racial and Ethnic Discrimination
Vol. 173 Sexual Health
Vol. 174 Selling Sex
Vol. 175 Citizenship and Participation
Vol. 176 Health Issues for Young People
Vol. 177 Crime in the UK
Vol. 178 Reproductive Ethics
Vol. 179 Tackling Child Abuse
Vol. 180 Money and Finances
Vol. 181 The Housing Issue

working mothers **107**.26; **154**.29
   and social housing **181**.10
working parents **107**.21-2, 24-5, 26
   effect on families **124**.1, 21
   role of father **124**.7-8, 11
workplace
   age discrimination **159**.8-13
   and disabled people **135**.15
   drug testing **128**.20
   exercise **162**.23, 24
   gambling **129**.22-4
   gender gap **154**.17-18
   obesity discrimination **162**.21
   monitoring **168**.9, 38
   racism **115**.11-14
   smoking ban **145**.14
   stress **165**.34
   travel plans **119**.32-3
workplace bullying **165**.32-9
   anti-bullying strategies **165**.35-6, 38
   costs **165**.39
   cyberbullying **165**.37-8
   e-mail **165**.38-9
   effects **165**.34, 35
   extent of **165**.33, 35
   preventing **165**.37
   signs of **165**.32, 25-6, 27
   what to do **165**.32
World Bank **157**.8, 10, 17
   help for developing countries in financial crisis **180**.1-2
world food supply, and GM crops **138**.9, 10, 34-5
world trade *see* international trade
World Trade Organisation (WTO) **88**.33; **157**.2-3, 8, 13-14, 17, 21-4
   and global water supplies **76**.5, 23
   and the liberalisation of water **76**.29
World Wide Web (WWW) **158**.2-3

Y

yoga **81**.3, 30, 39
   and back pain **162**.33-4
   and exam stress **100**.5
young children
   gender differences in achievements **154**.23
young offenders **177**.11-12
   and street homelessness **130**.11
young parents and non-traditional families **124**.20-21
young people
   and age discrimination **159**.12
   attitudes to biotechnology **138**.16
   attitudes to gun and knife crime **177**.15-16
   attitudes to HIV **164**.18
   attitudes to marriage **166**.1-2
   attitudes to mental ill-health **141**.25
   attitudes to police **177**.15-16
   bereavement support **116**.28
   and body image **170**.17
   and the Budget **180**.24
   and cannabis **163**.9, 30

   behavioural effects **128**.16
   possession **128**.27
   cannabis use **128**.6, 21
   education about risks **128**.28
   penalties for use **128**.9
as carers **135**.10-12
and citizenship *see* young people and citizenship
and cosmetic surgery **170**.32-3, 36
and crime *see* young offenders; youth crime
and criminal justice system **177**.16-18
and debt **134**.24
and depression **125**.8, 9
and divorce **124**.29-30, 34
and domestic abuse **155**.21, 26; **179**.19
and drug abuse **163**.3, 9, 15-16, 18-19; 26-30; **176**.18
and employment **180**.20
fear of **177**.3, 22
financial problems **180**.34-6
and funerals **116**.23
and gambling **129**.1
   gambling addiction **129**.25, 31, 32-3
   National Lottery **129**.11-13
   signs of problem gambling **129**.38
   views on gambling **129**.13
gang membership **177**.12-14
and gender violence **155**.21
and grief **116**.19-28
and healthy eating **88**.4; **176**.8-9
and HIV/AIDS **96**.17, 24-9, 38; **164**.18
homelessness *see* homeless young people
   improving profile of **177**.21
housing
   choosing to rent **181**.33
   living with parents **181**.4
   student housing **181**.18, 19-20
and the Internet **158**.27
   online gaming addiction **158**.39
   online risks **158**.28
media habits **142**.38
media representation **142**.15
and mental health **125**.16; **176**.29-39
and mental illness **141**.25
and money **180**.20-39
   financial awareness **180**.20-22
   financial education **180**.37-9
   financial outlook **180**.23
   financial problems **180**.34-6
   pension planning **159**.21
Muslims
   and fundamentalist beliefs **147**.16-17
   help to reject extremism **147**.34
and multi-faith environments **148**.32-3
news awareness **142**.32
and nutrition **176**.8-9
parenthood *see* teenage parents
parenting teenage children **124**.16-17
and the police **177**.15-16
and politics *see* young people and citizenship
poverty and mental illness **141**.22
and pregnancy *see* teenage pregnancies
relationships and domestic violence **179**.19

and religion **148**.34
rights **167**.28-39
and self-harm **136**.2, 4-19; **176**.33-5
and sex education development **133**.15-16
sexual exploitation of teenagers **99**.20-2
and sexual health **176**.21-8
and sexually transmitted infections (STIs) **96**.3, 4, 8-9,
   25; **133**.2-3, 12-13, 17; **176**.24-6
and smoking **145**.1, 2-6; **176**.3, 4, 12-13
   influence of films **145**.9-10
   nicotine patches **145**.20
and social exclusion **149**.38-9
and sport **118**.2
sport and self-esteem **170**.39
and suicide **136**.27-8
teenage girls
   breast augmentation **170**.32-3
   and domestic violence **155**.26
   sport and self-esteem **170**.39
unemployment **149**.38-9; **180**.34-5
and world trade **157**.17
young people and alcohol **176**.3, 4, 14-18
alcohol misuse **143**.29, 37
alcohol consumption **143**.2, 5, 15, 20, 37
binge drinking **176**.15-16
drinking habits **143**.2, 5, 15-17, 21, 37
eating problems **127**.20-21
exceeding daily benchmarks **143**.8
and HIV **96**.26
influence of others **143**.17
influence of television soaps **143**.18-19
and the law **143**.2, 17
obtaining alcohol **143**.16, 17, 20, 28
proposals to cut underage drinking **143**.5, 29
underage drinking **176**.17-18
underage purchase of alcohol **143**.16, 20, 28
young people and citizenship **131**.26-39
civic involvement **131**.31-2
and decision-making **131**.28
and the EU **131**.39
feelings of exclusion **131**.26
involvement in politics **131**.35
and mock elections **131**.27
political interest **131**.28, 31, 32, 35
political party support **131**.32
views on citizenship **131**.31-2
youth councils **131**.33-4
youth parliaments **131**.29, 33-4
Young People's Parliament (Birmingham) **131**.34
Young Scot **131**.34
youth councils **131**.33-4
youth courts **177**.16-18
youth crime **177**.9-22
costs **149**.39
gender differences **154**.25
public perceptions **177**.3, 20-21
trends **177**.20
see also young offenders
youth justice **177**.16-18
youth parliaments **131**.29, 33-4
youth unemployment **180**.34-5
costs of **149**.38-9
youth work
and extremism prevention **148**.30-31
interfaith **148**.33
single-sex **154**.5
YouTube **142**.35; **158**.21-2

Z

Zen Buddhism, and Kinhin (walking meditation) **100**.10
Zen macrobiotic diet **140**.2
zero carbon eco-towns **151**.32; **181**.36
zero-emission fuels **151**.28-9
zero waste initiatives **161**.7, 34
zinc **88**.6; **140**.3-4
zoo conservation **78**.24-50
zygote intrafallopian transfer (ZIFT) **178**.11

Volume numbers appear first (in bold) followed by page numbers; a change in volume number is preceded by a semi-colon.

Vol. 76 The Water Crisis	**Vol. 138** A Genetically Modified Future?	**Vol. 161** Waste Issues
Vol. 78 Threatened Species	**Vol. 139** The Education Problem	**Vol. 162** Staying Fit
Vol. 81 Alternative Therapies	**Vol. 140** Vegetarian and Vegan Diets	**Vol. 163** Drugs in the UK
Vol. 88 Food and Nutrition	**Vol. 141** Mental Health	**Vol. 164** The AIDS Crisis
Vol. 89 Refugees	**Vol. 142** Media Issues	**Vol. 165** Bullying Issues
Vol. 97 Energy Matters	**Vol. 143** Problem Drinking	**Vol. 166** Marriage and Cohabitation
Vol. 99 Exploited Children	**Vol. 144** The Cloning Debate	**Vol. 167** Our Human Rights
Vol. 100 Stress and Anxiety	**Vol. 145** Smoking Trends	**Vol. 168** Privacy and Surveillance
Vol. 107 Work Issues	**Vol. 146** Sustainability and Environment	**Vol. 169** The Animal Rights Debate
Vol. 116 Grief and Loss	**Vol. 147** The Terrorism Problem	**Vol. 170** Body Image and Self-Esteem
Vol. 118 Focus on Sport	**Vol. 148** Religious Beliefs	**Vol. 171** Abortion – Rights and Ethics
Vol. 119 Transport Trends	**Vol. 149** A Classless Society?	**Vol. 172** Racial and Ethnic Discrimination
Vol. 121 The Censorship Debate	**Vol. 150** Migration and Population	**Vol. 173** Sexual Health
Vol. 124 Parenting Issues	**Vol. 151** Climate Change	**Vol. 174** Selling Sex
Vol. 125 Understanding Depression	**Vol. 152** Euthanasia and the Right to Die	**Vol. 175** Citizenship and Participation
Vol. 127 Eating Disorders	**Vol. 153** Sexual Orientation and Society	**Vol. 176** Health Issues for Young People
Vol. 128 The Cannabis Issue	**Vol. 154** The Gender Gap	**Vol. 177** Crime in the UK
Vol. 129 Gambling Trends	**Vol. 155** Domestic Abuse	**Vol. 178** Reproductive Ethics
Vol. 130 Homelessness	**Vol. 156** Travel and Tourism	**Vol. 179** Tackling Child Abuse
Vol. 133 Teen Pregnancy and Lone Parents	**Vol. 157** The Problem of Globalisation	**Vol. 180** Money and Finances
Vol. 134 Customers and Consumerism	**Vol. 158** The Internet Revolution	**Vol. 181** The Housing Issue
Vol. 135 Coping with Disability	**Vol. 159** An Ageing Population	
Vol. 136 Self-Harm	**Vol. 160** Poverty and Exclusion	